I CAN RESIST EVERYTHING EXCEPT TEMPTATION

Famous Lines
The Columbia Dictionary of Familiar Quotations
by Robert Andrews

The Columbia Dictionary of Quotations
by Robert Andrews

Women's Words
The Columbia Book of Quotations by Women
by Mary Biggs

Family Wisdom
The 2,000 Most Important Things Ever Said about Parenting,
Children, and Family Life
by Susan Ginsberg

Of the People, By the People, For the People
And Other Quotations from Abraham Lincoln
by Gabor Borritt

When in Doubt, Tell the Truth
And Other Quotations from Mark Twain
by Brian Collins

Not Bloody Likely
And Other Quotations from Bernard Shaw
by Bernard Dukore

Hitch Your Wagon to a Star
And Other Quotations from Ralph Waldo Emerson
by Keith Frome

Simplify, Simplify
And Other Quotations from Henry David Thoreau
by K.P Van Anglen

I CAN RESIST EVERYTHING EXCEPT TEMPTATION

And Other Quotations from OSCAR WILDE

Karl Beckson

Columbia University Press

New York

Columbia University Press
Publishers Since 1893
New York   Chichester, West Sussex

Library of Congress Cataloging-in-Publication Data
   Wilde, Oscar, 1854–1900
   I can resist everything except temptation : and other quotations from
Oscar Wilde / [selected by] Karl Beckson.
      p.   cm.
   Includes bibliographical references (p.   ).
   ISBN 0-231-10456-1 (alk. paper)
   1. Wilde, Oscar, 1854–1900—Quotations. 2. Quotations, English—
Irish authors. I. Beckson, Karl E., 1926–. II. Title.
   PR5812.B43   1996   96-31894
   828'.809—dc20   CIP

Casebound editions of Columbia University Press books are printed on permanent and
durable acid-free paper.

Printed in the United States of America
c 10 9 8 7 6 5 4 3 2 1

Contents

Introduction   *xiii*
Key to Abbreviations   *xxi*

Quotations by Subject

Absinthe   1
Abstinence   1
Achievement   1
Action   1
Actors and Acting   2
Admiration   3
Advice   3
Aestheticism   3
Aesthetics   4
Affection   5
Agitators   5
Agreement   5
Altruism   6
Ambition   6
America and Americans   6
America: North   8
Analysis   8
Angels   9
Annunciation   9
Appearance   9
Archaeology   10
Arguments   10
Aristocracy   10
Arnold, Matthew   10
Art and Artists   11
Atonement   22
Australia   22
Authority   23

Autobiography   23

Bachelors   23
Bankruptcy   24
Beauty   24
Beerbohm, Max   25
Behavior   25
Belief   26
Books   26
Boredom   26
Brain, the   27
Bribery   27
Brothers   27
Browning, Elizabeth Barrett   28
Browning, Robert   28
Burial   30
Business   30
Byron, Lord   31

California   31
Cambridge University   32
Caricature   32
Cellini, Benvenuto   32
Celtic Poetry   33
Cemeteries   33
Certainty   33
Champagne   33
Change   34

Chaos 34
Character 35
Charity 35
Charm 35
Chicago 35
Children 36
Choices 36
Chopin, Frédéric 36
Christ 37
Cities 37
Civilization 38
Clergy 38
Cleverness 38
Commerce 39
Common Sense 39
Conceit 39
Confession 39
Conscience 40
Consistency 40
Consolation 40
Contemplation 41
Contradiction 41
Conversation 41
Conversion 42
Courage 42
Courtship 42
Cowardice 42
Creativity 43
Creditors 43
Crime 43
Crisis 44
Critics 44
Criticism 44
Crowds 46
Culture 46
Cure 47
Cynicism 47

Dancing 47
Dandyism 48

Dante 49
Darwin, Charles 49
Death 50
Debt 51
Debuts 51
Decadence 52
Decay 52
Degradation 52
Democracy 53
Despair 53
Despotism 53
Destiny 54
Dickens, Charles 54
Dilettantes 54
Disciples 55
Discontent 55
Dishonesty 55
Disobedience 55
Diversity 56
Divorce 56
Double Life 56
Dramatists 56
Dreamers 56
Dullness 57
Duty 57
Dying 58

Earnest 58
Eccentricity 58
Economics 58
Ecstasy 58
Education 59
Egotism 60
Elect, the 60
Emotions 60
Enemies 61
Engagements 61
England 61
English, the 63
Environment 65

Equality   65
Errors   65
Evil   66
Evolution   66
Examinations   66
Execution   67
Exercise   67
Experience   67
Experiment   67

Facts   68
Failures   68
Faithfulness   68
Fame   68
Family   69
Fate   69
Faults   69
Fiction   69
Fin de Siècle   70
Flaubert, Gustave   71
Flowers: Green   71
Fog   71
Folk-tale   71
Foreigners   72
Forgiveness   72
Form   72
France   73
Freedom   73
Friends   74
Friendship   74

Generosity   75
Genius   75
Geniuses   75
Gide, André   76
God   76
Gods, the   76
Goethe, Johann von   76
Goodness   77
Gossip   77

Government   77
Graves   78
Greek Dramatists   78
Greek Tragedy   78
Greek Art   79
Grief   79

Haggard, Rider   79
Handicrafts   79
Happiness   80
Health   80
Heaven   80
Hedonism   80
Hellenism   81
Heroes   81
Heroism   82
History   82
Holy Family, the   83
Homosexuality   83
Honor   83
Hostesses   84
Houses and Homes   84
Hughes, Willie   84
Humanism   85
Humanity   85
Humility   85
Husbands   85
Huysmans, Joris-Karl   86

Ideal Man   86
Idealism: Greek   87
Idealism   87
Ideas   87
Identities   88
Idleness   88
Ignorance   88
Imitation   88
Impressionism   89
Imprisonment   89
Incredibility   89

Indifference   89
Individualism   90
Influence   91
Information   91
Injustice   91
Insincerity   92
Intellectual Life   92
Ireland   92
Irish, the   93
Irving, Henry   93

James, Henry   93
Journalism   93

Keats, John   94
Kindness   96
Kipling, Rudyard   96
Knowledge   97

Labor   97
Langtry, Lillie   98
Language   98
Language: German   99
Laughter   99
Law   100
Legends   100
Liars   100
Life   100
Listening   104
Literature   104
London   104
Longfellow, Henry Wadsworth   104
Love   105
Lying   107

Marriage   108
Marriage: Proposals   109
Martyrdom   109
Masterpiece   110
Maupassant, Guy de   110

Mediaevalism   110
Mediocrity   110
Melodrama   111
Men and Women   111
Men   115
Men: American   115
Meredith, George   115
Michelangelo   116
Milton, John   116
Miracles   116
Misfortune   117
Missionaries   117
Moderation   117
Modern Times   118
Modernity   118
Money   119
Moon, the   119
Moore, George   119
Moral   119
Moralists   120
Morality   120
Morbidity   121
Morris, William   121
Mourning   121
Murder   122
Music   123
Mystery   123

Names   123
Narcissism   124
Nature   125
New York   127
Niagara Falls   127
Night   127
Nightingale   128
Nonsense   128

Objectivity   128
Occupations   128
Old Age   129

Opinions   129
Optimism   129
Origins   130
Oxford University   130

Pain   130
Painters   131
Painting   131
Pantheism   131
Papacy and Popes   132
Paradox   132
Parents   133
Parody   133
Passion   133
Past, the   134
Pater, Walter   134
Pathology   135
Peerage   136
People   136
People, the   136
Perfection   137
Personality   137
Pessimism   138
Philanthropist   138
Pity   138
Platitudes   139
Pleasure   139
Poe, Edgar Allan   139
Poetry   140
Poets   141
Politics   142
Popularity   142
Portraits   143
Prayer   143
Pre-Raphaelites   143
Preaching   144
Pretension   144
Price   145
Principles   145
Prison and Prisoners   145

Professions   146
Property   147
Prose   147
Prostitution   148
Prudence   148
Psychology   148
Public, the   148
Punishment   149
Puppets   149
Puritanism   149
Purity   149

Reading   150
Realism   150
Rebirth   150
Recognition   151
Reflections   151
Rejection   151
Relations   151
Religion   152
Renaissance   152
Reputation   153
Resolve   153
Revising   153
Rhyme   153
Rituals: Religious   154
Romance   154
Romanticism   155
Rossetti, Christina   155
Ruin   156
Running Away   156
Ruskin, John   156

Sacredness   157
Sacrilege   157
Saints   158
Salomé   158
Sand, George   158
Scandals   159
Scholarship   159

Schools   159
Schopenhauer, Arthur   160
Science   160
Secrets   160
Self, the   162
Selfishness   162
Senses   162
Sentimentality   163
Separation   163
Sex   164
Shakespeare   164
Shallowness   165
Shelley, Percy Bysshe   165
Similarity   166
Sin   166
Sincerity   167
Skepticism   167
Slavery   167
Socialism   167
Society   168
Sorrow   170
Soul, the   170
Spectator   171
Speculation   171
Spirituality   171
St. Francis of Assisi   172
Staring   172
State, the   172
Stevenson, Robert Louis   172
Stupidity   173
Style   173
Success   173
Suffering   174
Suicide   174
Sunset   174
Superficiality   175
Superstition   175

Surprise   175
Survival   175
Suspense   175
Swinburne, Algernon Charles   176
Switzerland   176
Sympathy   176

Talking   177
Temperament   178
Temptation   178
Terror   179
Terry, Ellen   179
Theater   179
Theories   179
Town   180
Tragedies   180
Transcendentalism   181
Travel   182
Trials   182
Triviality   182
Truth   182
Turgenev, Ivan   184

Ugliness   184
Underclass, the   185
Utilitarianism   186
Utopia   186

Vanity   187
Venus de Milo   187
Vision   187

Wagner, Richard   187
Wainewright, Thomas Griffiths
   188
Waiting   188
War   188

Watson, William   189
Weak, the   189
Wealth   189
Weariness   189
Weather, the   190
Western World   190
Whistler, James McNeill   190
Whitman, Walt   192
Wickedness   192
Wild Oats   193
Winter, John Strange   193

Women   194
Women: American   194
Work   196
Worship   196
Writing: Russian   196
Writing   196

Yeats, William Butler   197
Youth   197

Zola, Emile   198

*I*NTRODUCTION

The first paradox, it is said, was made in the Garden of Eden when God created man in His own image. In the great tradition of paradox creators, Oscar Wilde (1854–1900), according to Ernest Newman in the *Free Review* (June 1, 1895), may be regarded as having advanced paradox as "simply the truth of the minority, just as a commonplace is the truth of the majority. . . . We ordinary beings can see objects in three dimensions only; a good paradox is a view in the fourth dimension." In short, a paradox belongs to a world "that never existed." In hearing or reading paradoxes, we "rise from the perusal of them with a self-conscious wisdom that we had not before. We become wise, and know it: and that is the only sort of wisdom worth having."

The term *paradox*, derived from Greek, means the expression of a view contrary to received opinion or expectation. As a clash of contradictory views, the paradox is closely allied to the oxymoron, which also involves contradiction though with its terms intimately joined, as in Romeo's "O loving hate!" Both the paradox and oxymoron, while seeming to express contradictions, simultaneously reveal a basic truth—the nature of human ambivalence. Wilde so brilliantly embodied paradoxes in epigrams that, to this day, they provide us with discoveries of that "fourth dimension" described by Newman. One of Wilde's devices for unsettling his readers was to invert bourgeois commonplaces, as in the following from *The Picture of Dorian Gray* (1891), probably the wittiest novel in the language: "When we are happy we are always good, but when we are good we are not always happy."

In the novel, Lord Henry Wotton, who is called "Prince Paradox," is adept, as was Wilde, in evoking the "fourth dimension": "He played with the idea, and grew wilful; tossed it into the air and transformed it; let it escape and recaptured it; made it iridescent with fancy, and winged it with paradox." Having observed Lord Henry, one character concludes that "the way of paradoxes is the way of truth. To test Reality we must see it on the tight rope. When the verities become acrobats, we can judge them." Indeed, to confirm this view, Wilde wrote in his essay "The Truth of Masks" (1891): "A Truth in art is that whose contradictory is also true."

Since, for Wilde, a truth in art involves both elements of a contradiction, in his society drama *An Ideal Husband* (1895), an exchange between the dandy Lord Goring and his father, Lord Caversham, illustrates that paradoxes may be rejected in favor of other paradoxes, an indication that some acrobats are more adept than others on the tightrope:

LORD GORING: If there was less sympathy in the world there would be less
   trouble in the world.
LORD CAVERSHAM: That is a paradox, sir. I hate paradoxes.
LORD GORING: So do I, father. Everybody one meets is a paradox nowadays.
   It is a great bore. It makes society so obvious.

Though Wilde's life and career were filled with paradoxes, he was certainly neither boring nor obvious. Indeed, he was, by all accounts, wittier in conversation than he was in his works. From his days as an Oxford student (1874–78), he amused his fellow students as an idle poseur while deeply involved in his studies and his poetry, winning, in his final year, the prestigious Newdigate Prize for his long poem *Ravenna* (published on the day of the award) and achieving a B.A. degree with a double First. He later wrote to a friend of his fond memories of Oxford: "I remember bright young faces, and grey misty quadrangles, Greek forms passing through Gothic cloisters, life playing among ruins, and, what I loved best in the world, Poetry and Paradox dancing together!"

His 1882 lecture tour of the United States and Canada, arranged by the impresario Richard D'Oyly Carte, brought him fame as he appeared, initially, in aesthetic costume to advertise Gilbert and Sullivan's *Patience*, then being performed in America. His bright sayings, such as the reported response to a customs official—"I have nothing to declare except my genius"—revealed his striking, memorable wit. Though his lectures advanced, with some seriousness, the intent of the Aesthetic Movement, his interviews with newspaper reporters provided opportunities for advancing his reputation as a wit. To a reporter in the Halifax *Morning Herald*, Wilde confided his adoration of the actress Lillie Langtry: "I would rather have discovered Mrs. Langtry than have discovered America." During his lecture tour, when he was widely satirized in the press, he reportedly remarked: "I am sad because half the world does not believe in God, and the other half does not believe in me."

If his lecture tour of America revealed Wilde's capacity for showmanship despite the earnestness of his aestheticism, the publication of *The Picture of Dorian Gray* erupted in critical attacks not only for its suggestions of homoeroticism but also for its startling paradoxes. However, Nathaniel Hawthorne, son of the novelist, wrote in *Lippincott's Monthly Magazine* (Sept. 1890), in which the first version of the novel had appeared, that some of Wilde's "clever sayings are more than clever—they show real insight and a comprehensive grasp." And the noted critic Walter Pater, in the most perceptive review of the enlarged version of the novel, wrote approvingly: "His genial, laughter-loving sense of life and its enjoyable intercourse, goes far to obviate any crudity there may be in the paradox . . . with the bright and shining truth which often underlies it. . . ."

In 1891, Wilde published not only the book version of *Dorian Gray* but also his volume of revised critical essays titled *Intentions*. As a critical thinker, Wilde was generally hailed for his epigrammatic style, particularly for his perceptive essay, in the form of a dialogue, titled "The Decay of Lying": "What Art really reveals to us is Nature's lack of design, her curious crudities, her extraordinary monotony, her absolutely unfinished condition." Moreover, the essay advances a striking proposition: "Paradox though it may seem—and paradoxes are always dangerous things—it is none the less true that life imitates art far more than art imitates life." In *United Ireland* (Sept. 26, 1891), W. B. Yeats said of the volume that "it hides within its immense paradox some of the most subtle literary criticism we are likely to see for many a long day." In the *Speaker* (July 4, 1891), the critic Arthur Symons, describing Wilde as "much too brilliant to be ever believed" and "much too witty to be ever taken seriously," praises the "paradoxical truths" of the volume:

By constantly saying the opposite of sensible opinions, he proves to us that opposites can often be equally true. While he insists on producing his paradox, sometimes for no other reason than that it is a paradox, and would rather say something that is clever than something that is merely true, it is surprising . . . how often he succeeds in combining truth and cleverness.

In the *North American Review* (Jan. 1892), the American essayist and biographer Agnes Repplier cited *Intentions* as "The Best Book of the Year:"

"... few there are who listen to [Wilde], partly because his philosophy is alien to our prevalent modes of thought, and partly because of the perverse and paradoxical fashion in which he delights to give it utterance."

Having demonstrated in *Dorian Gray* and in *Intentions* that he was one of the great wits of the century in fiction and in criticism, Wilde proceeded to convince the general public, if not some of his carping critics, that he was also capable of writing some of the wittiest plays in the history of British drama in his epigrammatic style, fusing the wisdom of the "fourth dimension" with the subversive laughter associated with the dandies in his four society dramas, beginning with *Lady Windermere's Fan* (1892) and concluding with *The Importance of Being Earnest* (1895), his masterpiece. Reviewing *Lady Windermere's Fan*, A. B. Walkley, enormously impressed, wrote in the *Speaker* (Feb. 27):

If we have had more sparkling dialogue on the stage in the present generation, I have not heard it. . . . All the men talk like Mr. Oscar Wilde. Everything is discussed paradoxically, from the connection between London fogs and seriousness—"whether London fogs produce the serious people or serious people the London fogs"—to the connection between feminine frivolty and feminine charms—"nothing is so unbecoming to a woman as a Nonconformist conscience"; from cynicism—"the cynic is the man who knows the price of everything and the value of nothing"—to married womanhood—"nothing is so glorious in life as the devotion of a married woman; it is a subject about which no married man knows anything."

However, one of Wilde's critics in the theatrical newspaper *Black and White* (Feb. 27) voiced what became a common complaint by some critics of his plays: ". . . it is obvious that Mr. Wilde regards a play as a vehicle merely for the expression of epigram and the promulgation of paradox. *Lady Windermere's Fan* is not really a play; it is a pepper-box of paradoxes."

In reviewing Wilde's second society drama, *A Woman of No Importance* (1893) in the *World* (April 26), William Archer, the noted drama critic and translator of Ibsen, helped to establish Wilde's reputation in the theater: ". . . the one essential fact about Mr. Oscar Wilde's dramatic work is that it must be taken on the very highest plane of modern English drama, and furthermore, that it stands alone on that plane." Despite such praise, Archer was uneasy about Wilde's inclination to "trifle gracefully with his art"—an allusion to his "pyrotechnic wit." In the *Speaker* (April 29), Walkley agreed with Archer that Wilde, in his play, included too many epigrams: "After a half-a-dozen or so, anyone can see through the trick; and when they cease to surprise, they cease to amuse." The anonymous review in the *Saturday Review* (May 6) was even harsher in its view of Wilde's penchant for epigrammatic dialogue in the dandy, Lord Illingworth, who, writes the critic, is "not quite human, and is little more than a machine for the utterance of paradox and epigram, most of them, though by no means all, wonderfully clever, but bearing upon them the hall-mark of insincerity."

Having praised *A Woman of No Importance*, Archer, in the *Pall Mall Budget* (10 Jan. 1895), regarded Wilde's next play, *An Ideal Husband* (1895), as "a very able and entertaining piece of work, charmingly written . . . but there are times when the output of Mr. Wilde's epigram-factory threatens to become all trademark and no substance." Nevertheless, Archer finds in this play, as in Wilde's other plays, "one really profound saying, which serves to mark it in my memory" (in short, as Newman suggested, a view of the "fourth dimension"): "Vulgarity is the behaviour of other people." In the *Speaker* (Jan. 12), Walkley, who had been impressed by *Lady Windermere's Fan*, was highly critical of *An Ideal Husband* in the lack of moral tone of Wilde's "romantically absurd view of political life," derived, Walkley might have added, from popular French well-made plays. Wilde's epigrammatic style, writes Walkley, consisting of "inverted commonplaces, are Mr. Wilde's distinctive mark . . . and the best that can be said for *An Ideal Husband* is that in it the output of them is considerably diminished." Bernard Shaw, in his droll review in the *Saturday Review* (Jan. 12), regards the play as

a dangerous subject, because [Wilde] has the property of making his critics dull. They laugh angrily at his epigrams, like a child who is coaxed into being amused in the very act of setting up a yell of rage and agony. They protest that the trick is obvious, and that such epigrams can be turned out by the score by any one lightminded enough to condescend to such frivolity. As far as I can ascertain, I am the only person in London who cannot sit down and write an Oscar Wilde play at will.

Wilde's final play, *The Importance of Being Earnest*, produced just a month after *An Ideal Husband*, received very favorable reviews, though Shaw's, in the *Saturday Review* (Feb. 23, 1895), revealed an ambivalence based on the play's refusal to take social problems seriously: "I cannot say that I greatly cared for *The Importance of Being Earnest*. It amused me, of course, but unless comedy touches me as well as amuses me, it leaves me with a sense of having wasted my evening." In the *Speaker* (Feb. 23), however, Walkley declared that Wilde had " 'found himself' at last, as an artist in sheer nonsense . . . and better nonsense, I think, our stage has not seen." And in the *World* (20 Feb.), Archer regarded the play as "an absolutely wilful expression of an irrepressibly witty personality." An uncanny prediction is expressed by the anonymous reviewer in *Truth* (Feb. 21), who writes that "days of the 'Paradox *à la* Wilde' may be numbered." Indeed, they were, for in early April, Wilde was arrested for committing "acts of gross indecency with another male person," tried twice (the first trial resulting in a hung jury), and, on May 25, sentenced to two years at hard labor (1895-97).

The paradox of a renowned man of letters at the height of his fame, glorying in the simultaneous production of two of his wittiest dramas playing to packed houses at the time of his arrest, dramatizes the extraordinary career of Oscar Wilde. At the time of the trials, William Archer wrote to his brother: "Really the luck is against the poor British drama—the man who has more brains in his little finger than all the rest of them in their whole body goes and commits worse than suicide in this way."

In *De Profundis*, his prison letter to Lord Alfred Douglas, his young lover, Wilde evaluated the extraordinary achievement of his brief career:

I took the drama, the most objective form known to art, and made it as personal a mode of expression as the lyric or the sonnet. . . . I treated Art as the supreme reality, and life as a mere mode of fiction: I awoke the imagination of my century so that it created myth and legend around me: I summed up all systems in a phrase, and all existence in an epigram.

At the same time, he acknowledged the existence of paradox in one's own life, as he wrote in the same letter to Douglas: "To be entirely free, and at the same time entirely dominated by law is the eternal paradox of human life that we realise at every moment. . . ." Even at the time of his death, he remained the observer of his own paradoxical extravagance: "I am dying, as I have lived, beyond my means," he reportedly said.

Many of Wilde's epigrams and paradoxes remain as strikingly original today as when he first fashioned them. Dorothy Parker, known for her acerbic wit, acknowledged their brilliance in her brief tribute to Wilde:

If, with the literate, I am
Impelled to try an epigram,
I never seek to take the credit;
We all assume that Oscar said it.

A NOTE ON THE TEXT

Dialogue from Wilde's fiction is presented with speakers' names as though in a printed play—that is, with descriptive details omitted, such as "murmured Dorian, with his eyes still fixed upon his own portrait." Unless otherwise indicated, all books, periodicals, and newspapers cited herein were published in London.

*K*EY *TO ABBREVIATIONS*

Collected Edition	*Collected Edition of the Works of Oscar Wilde*, 14 vols. Ed. Robert Ross (1908; repr. in 1993).
CSR	*Court and Society Review.*
De Profundis	Partly pub. in 1905. Ed. Robert Ross, who also pub. *The Suppressed Portion of "De Profundis"* (New York, 1913), which contains material never before published.
Dorian Gray	*The Picture of Dorian Gray. Lippincott's Monthly Magazine* (London and Philadelphia, July 1890); rev., enlarged book version, with a Preface and six new chapters, 1891.
Duchess	*The Duchess of Padua.* Privately printed in 1883; produced in New York, in Jan. 1891.
Earnest	*The Importance of Being Earnest.* Produced Feb. 1895; pub. in 1899.
Ellmann	Richard Ellmann, ed. *The Artist as Critic: Critical Writings of Oscar Wilde* (New York, 1969).
"English Renaissance"	"The English Renaissance of Art." Wilde's lecture given in America, 1882; pub. in *Miscellanies.*
Fan	*Lady Windermere's Fan.* Produced in Feb. 1892; pub. in 1893.
"A Few Maxims"	"A Few Maxims for the Instruction of the Over-Educated." *Saturday Review* (Nov. 17 1894); repr. in *Letters*, Appendix B.
FR	*Fortnightly Review.* Gide, André. *Oscar Wilde: A Study*, trans. Stuart Mason (1905). First pub. in *L'Ermitage* (Paris, June 1902).
The Happy Prince	*The Happy Prince and Other Tales* (1888); repr. in Vol. 10 of the *Collected Edition.*

Harris	Frank Harris, *Oscar Wilde: His Life and Confessions*, 2 vols. (New York, 1916).
"Historical Criticism"	"The Rise of Historical Criticism." Parts 1-3 pub. in Vol. 7, *Lord Arthur Savile's Crime and Other Prose Pieces*, of the *Collected Edition*; part 4 pub. in Vol. 14, *Miscellanies*.
Housman	Laurence Housman. *Echo de Paris* (1923).
Husband	*An Ideal Husband*. Produced in Jan. 1895; pub. in 1899.
Hyde	H. Montgomery Hyde. *Three Trials of Oscar Wilde* (New York, 1973).
Letters	*The Letters of Oscar Wilde*. Ed. Rupert Hart-Davis (New York, 1962).
Lewis and Smith	Lloyd Lewis and Henry Justin Smith. *Oscar Wilde Discovers America*, 1882 (New York, 1936; repr. New York, 1967).
Lord Arthur	*Lord Arthur Savile's Crime & Other Stories* (1891); repr. as *Lord Arthur Savile's Crime and Other Prose Pieces* in Vol. 7 of the *Collected Edition*.
Mason	Stuart Mason. *Bibliography of Oscar Wilde* (1914; repr. 1967).
Mikhail	E. H. Mikhail, ed. *Oscar Wilde: Interviews and Recollections*, 2 vols. (London and New York, 1978).
Miscellanies	Vol. 14 of the *Collected Edition*.
More Letters	*More Letters of Oscar Wilde*. Ed. Rupert Hart-Davis (New York, 1985).
Mr. W. H.	*The Portrait of Mr. W. H.* (New York, 1921); repr. in Ellmann. A briefer version of the story had appeared in *Blackwood's Edinburgh Magazine* (July 1889).
O'Brien	Kevin O'Brien. *Oscar Wilde in Canada* (Toronto, 1982). Includes reconstructions from newspaper accounts of "The Decorative Arts" and "The House Beautiful," Wilde's 1882 lectures in America.

"Phrases and Philosophies"   "Phrases and Philosophies for the Use of Young." *Chameleon* (Oxford, Dec. 1894); repr. in Ellmann.

PMG   *Pall Mall Gazette.*

Poems (1908)   Vol. 9 of the *Collected Edition.*

Poems (1997)   *Poems and Poems in Prose.* Ed. Bobby Fong and Karl Beckson (Oxford and New York, 1997). Vol. 4 of *The Complete Works of Oscar Wilde.* Gen. ed. Russell Jackson and Ian Small.

Reading Gaol   *The Ballad of Reading Gaol* (1898); repr. in *Poems* (1997).

Reviews   Vol. 13 of the *Collected Edition.*

Small   Ian Small. *Oscar Wilde Revalued* (Greensboro, NC, 1993).

Smith and Helfand   Philip Smith and Michael Helfand, ed. *Oscar Wilde's Oxford Notebooks* (New York, 1989). Contains Wilde's "Commonplace Book" and "Notebook."

"The Soul of Man"   "The Soul of Man under Socialism." First pub. in *FR* (Feb. 1891); repr. in Ellmann.

Vera   *Vera; or, The Nihilists.* Privately printed in 1880; produced in August 1883 in New York.

A Woman   *A Woman of No Importance.* Produced in April 1893; pub. in 1894.

Wyndham   Violet Wyndham. *The Sphinx and Her Circle: A Biographical Sketch of Ada Leverson* (London and New York, 1963). Includes Leverson's "Reminiscences" from *Letters to the Sphinx from Oscar Wilde* (1930).

$\mathcal{A}$BSINTHE

After the first glass, you see things as you wish they were. After the second, you see them as they are not. Finally you see things as they really are, and that is the most horrible thing in the world.

> Quoted in: "Reminiscences" by Ada Leverson, repr. in Wyndham, 117.
> On the effects of absinthe.

$\mathcal{A}$BSTINENCE

Self-denial is the shining sore on the leprous body of Christianity.

> Quoted in: Harris, ch. 24.

$\mathcal{A}$CHIEVEMENT

A man's very highest moment is, I have no doubt at all, when he kneels in the dust, and beats his breast, and tells all the sins of his life.

> *Letters*, 502.
> Written to Alfred Douglas in early 1897 from Reading Prison, partly pub. as *De Profundis* (1905).

$\mathcal{A}$CTION

Action, indeed, is always easy, and when presented to us in its most aggravated, because most continuous form, which I take to be that of real industry, becomes simply the refuge of people who have nothing whatsoever to do.

> Gilbert in "The Critic as Artist," pt. 1, in *Intentions* (1891), repr. in Ellmann, 359.

If we lived long enough to see the results of our actions it may be that those who call themselves good would be sickened with a dull remorse, and those whom the world calls evil stirred by a noble joy. Each little thing that we do passes into the great machine of life which may grind our virtues to powder and make them worthless, or transform our sins into elements of a new civilization. . . .

Gilbert in "The Critic as Artist," pt. 1, in *Intentions* (1891), repr. in Ellmann, 369.

More difficult to do a thing than to talk about it? Not at all. That is a gross popular error. It is very much more difficult to talk about a thing than to do it. In the sphere of actual life that is of course obvious. Anybody can make history. Only a great man can write it.

Gilbert in "The Critic as Artist," pt. 1, in *Intentions* (1891), repr. in Ellmann, 359.

No, Ernest, don't talk about action. It is a blind thing dependent on external influences, and moved by an impulse of whose nature it is unconscious. . . . Its basis is the lack of imagination. It is the last resource of those who know not how to dream.

Gilbert in "The Critic as Artist," pt. 1, in *Intentions* (1891), repr. in Ellmann, 359.

When man acts he is a puppet. When he describes he is a poet. The whole secret lies in that. It was easy enough on the sandy plains by windy Ilion to send the notched arrow from the painted bow, or to hurl against the shield of hide and flake-like brass the long ash-handled spear. . . . But what of those who wrote about these things? What of those who gave them reality, and made them live forever? Are they not greater than the men and women they sing of?

Gilbert in "The Critic as Artist," pt. 1, in *Intentions* (1891), repr. in Ellmann, 361.

Ilion is also known as Troy.

$\mathcal{A}$CTORS *AND* ACTING

People sometimes say that actors give us their own Hamlets, and not Shakespeare's. . . . In point of fact, there is no such thing as Shakespeare's Hamlet. If Hamlet has something of the definiteness of a work of art, he has also all the obscurity that belongs to life. There are as many Hamlets as there are melancholies.

Gilbert in "The Critic as Artist," pt. 2, in *Intentions* (1891), repr. in Ellmann, 374.

As a rule, people who act lead the most commonplace lives. They are good husbands, or faithful wives, or something tedious. You know what I mean—middle-class virtue, and all that kind of thing. How different Sibyl was! She lived her finest tragedy. She was always a heroine.

Dorian to Basil Hallward in *Dorian Gray*, ch. 9.

On Sibyl Vane after her suicide.

The mere mechanical *technique* of acting can be taught, but the spirit that is to give life to lifeless forms must be born in a man. No dramatic college can teach its pupils to think or to feel. It is Nature who makes our artists for us, though it may be Art who taught them their right mode of expression.

"*The Winter's Tale* at the Lyceum," in *CSR* (September 14, 1887), repr. in Mason, 43.

$\mathcal{A}$DMIRATION

The reason we all like to think so well of others is that we are all afraid for ourselves. The basis of optimism is sheer terror.

Lord Henry in *Dorian Gray*, ch. 6.

$\mathcal{A}$DVICE

I always pass on good advice. It is the only thing to do with it. It is never of any use to oneself.

Lord Goring in *Husband*, act 1.

$\mathcal{A}$ESTHETICISM

We have got rid of what was bad. We have now to make what is beautiful. And though the mission of the aesthetic movement is to lure people to contemplate, not to lead them to create, yet, as the creative instinct is strong in the Celt, and it is the Celt who leads in art, there is no reason why in future years this strange Renaissance should not become almost as

mighty in its way as was that new birth of Art that woke many centuries
ago in the cities of Italy.

> Gilbert in "The Critic as Artist," pt. 2, in *Intentions* (1891), repr. in Ellmann, 396.

I feel that the entire subordination in our aesthetic movement of all merely
emotional and intellective motives to the vital, informing poetic principle
is the surest sign of our strength.

> "L'Envoi," in Rennell Rodd's *Rose Leaf and Apple Leaf* (Philadelphia, 1882), repr. in *Miscellanies*, 35.

Oh, would that I could live up to my blue china!

> Quoted in: Robert Sherard's *The Life of Oscar Wilde* (New York, 1906), ch. 7.
>
> Blue china was esteemed among the Aesthetes of the 1870s.

How often I feel how hard it is to live up to my blue china.

> Quoted in: *Oxford and Cambridge Undergraduate's Journal* (February 27, 1879), repr. in Richard
> Ellmann, *Oscar Wilde* (New York, 1988), 45.
>
> In *Punch* (October 1880), George du Maurier's cartoon titled "The Six-mark Tea-pot" depicts an
> "Intense Bride," who, while holding the tea-pot, says to her "Aesthetic Bridegroom"
> (resembling Wilde): "...Oh, Algernon, let us live up to it!"

*A*ESTHETICS

Aesthetics are higher than ethics. They belong to a more spiritual sphere.
To discern the beauty of a thing is the finest point to which we can arrive.
Even a colour-sense is more important, in the development of the
individual, than a sense of right and wrong.

> Gilbert in "The Critic as Artist," pt. 2, in *Intentions* (1891), repr. in Ellmann, 406.

Aesthetics, in fact, are to Ethics in the sphere of conscious civilization,
what, in the sphere of the external world, sexual is to natural selection.
Ethics, like natural selection, make existence possible. Aesthetics, like sexual
selection, make life lovely and wonderful, fill it with new forms, and give it
progress, and variety and change.

> Gilbert in "The Critic as Artist," pt. 2, in *Intentions* (1891), repr. in Ellmann, 406.

I look forward to the time when aesthetics will take the place of ethics,
when the sense of beauty will be the dominant law of life: it will never be
so, and so I look forward to it.

> *Letters*, 265.
>
> Written to Mrs. Bertha Lathbury, an acquaintance, in the summer of 1890.

Begin by changing the name of your town.

Quoted in: Henri Mazel's "My Recollections of Oscar Wilde," *Everyman* (October 18, 1912), repr. in Mikhail, 2:446.

During his American lecture tour, Wilde received an invitation from Griggsville, Kansas, to lecture on aesthetics; he wired his response given above.

$\mathcal{A}$FFECTION

CARSON: Did you ever kiss him?
WILDE: Oh, dear no! He was a peculiarly plain boy. He was, unfortunately, extremely ugly. I pitied him for it.
CARSON: Was that the reason why you did not kiss him?
WILDE: Oh! Mr. Carson: you are pertinently insolent.

Quoted in: Hyde, 133-34.

An exchange between the barrister Edward Carson and Wilde concerning Wilde's behavior with a young man that changed the course of the April 1895 libel trial involving the Marquess of Queensberry, who had charged Wilde with "posing" as a sodomite.

$\mathcal{A}$GITATORS

What is said by great employers of labour against agitators is unquestionably true. Agitators are a set of interfering, meddling people, who come down to some perfectly contented class of the community, and sow the seeds of discontent amongst them. That is the reason why agitators are so absolutely necessary. Without them, in our incomplete state, there would be no advance towards civilization.

"The Soul of Man," repr. in Ellmann, 259.

$\mathcal{A}$GREEMENT

Ah! Don't say that you agree with me. When people agree with me I always feel that I must be wrong.

Gilbert in "The Critic as Artist," pt. 2, in *Intentions* (1891), repr. in Ellmann, 401.

The aphorism reappears in Cecil Graham's remarks in *Fan*, act 3.

$\mathcal{A}$LTRUISM

We have had the spectacle of men who have really studied the problem [of poverty] and know the life—educated men who in the East-end—coming forward and imploring the community to restrain its altruistic impulses of charity, benevolence, and the like. They do so on the ground that such charity degrades and demoralizes. They are perfectly right. Charity creates a multitude of sins.

"The Soul of Man," repr. in Ellmann 256.

$\mathcal{A}$MBITION

Ambition, love and all the thoughts that burn
We lose too soon, and only find delight
In withered husks of some dead memory.

"Désespoir," unpublished in Wilde's lifetime, appears in *Poems* (1997).
The title means "Despair".

Ambition is the last refuge of the failure.

"Phrases and Philosophies," repr. in Ellmann, 434.

$\mathcal{A}$MERICA AND AMERICANS

In America the young are always ready to give to those who are older than themselves the full benefits of their inexperience.

"The American Invasion," in *CSR* (March 23, 1887), repr. in Ellmann, 56.

America has never quite forgiven Europe for having been discovered somewhat earlier in history than itself. Yet how immense are its obligations to us! How enormous its debt!

"The American Man," in *CSR* (April 13, 1887), repr. in Ellmann, 63.

In America, the horrors of domesticity are almost entirely unknown. There are no scenes over the soup, nor quarrels over the *entrées*, and as, by a clause inserted in every marriage settlement, the husband solemnly

binds himself to use studs and not buttons for his shirts, one of the chief
sources of disagreement in ordinary middle-class life is absolutely
removed.

"The American Man," in *CSR* (April 13, 1887), repr. in Ellmann, 62.

The crude commercialism of America, its materialising spirit, its
indifference to the poetical side of things, and its lack of imagination and
of high unattainable ideals, are entirely due to that country having adopted
for its national hero a man, who according to his own confession, was
incapable of telling a lie, and it is not too much to say that the story of
George Washington and the cherry-tree has done more harm, and in a
shorter space of time, than any other moral tale in the whole of literature.

Vivian in "The Decay of Lying," in *Intentions* (1891), repr. in Ellmann, 304.

She behaves as if she was beautiful. Most American women do. It is the
secret of their charm.

Lord Henry in *Dorian Gray*, ch. 3.
Commenting on the fiancée of a friend.

SIR THOMAS BURDON: The Americans are an extremely interesting people.
They are absolutely reasonable. . . . I assure you there is no nonsense
about the Americans.
LORD HENRY: How dreadful! I can stand brute force, but brute reason is
quite unbearable. There is something unfair about its use. It is hitting
below the intellect.

Dorian Gray, ch. 3.

SIR THOMAS BURDON: They say that when good Americans die they go to
Paris. . . .
LADY AGATHA: Really! And where do bad Americans go to when they die?
LORD HENRY: They go to America. . . .

Dorian Gray, ch. 3, the passage repeated in *A Woman*, act 1.

America is the noisiest country that ever existed. One is waked up in the
morning, not by the singing of the nightingale, but by the steam whistle.

Impressions of America, ed. Stuart Mason (Sunderland, 1906), repr. in Ellmann, 7.

LADY CAROLINE: These American girls carry off all the good matches. Why
can't they stay in their own country? They are always telling us it is the
Paradise of women.

LORD ILLINGWORTH: It is, Lady Caroline. That is why, like Eve, they are so extremely anxious to get out of it.

A Woman, act 1.

LADY CAROLINE: There are a great many things you haven't got in America, I am told, Miss Worsley. They say you have no ruins, and no curiosities. MRS. ALLONBY: What nonsense! They have their mothers and their manners.

A Woman, act 2.

When I landed in New York and read what the newspapers had to say about me, I thought I was about to travel in an extensive lunatic asylum, but when I went out in society there, I found the most charming cosmopolitan people I ever had the pleasure of meeting.

Quoted in: Lewis and Smith, 336.

In an interview, in April 1882, with a *Topeka Capital* reporter.

*A*MERICA: NORTH

When I was in America, I did not dare to tell America the truth; but I saw it clearly even then—that the discovery of America was the beginning of the death of Art.

Quoted in: Housman, 27.

*A*NALYSIS

The more one analyses people, the more all reasons for analysis disappear. Sooner or later one comes to that dreadful universal thing called human nature. Indeed, as any one who has ever worked among the poor knows only too well, the brotherhood of man is no mere poet's dream, it is a most depressing and humiliating reality. . . .

Vivian in "The Decay of Lying," in *Intentions* (1891), repr. in Ellmann, 297.

ANGELS

Get thee behind me! I hear in the palace the beating of the wings of the angel of death. . . . Angel of the Lord God, what dost thou here with thy sword? Whom seekest thou in this palace? The day of him who shall die in a robe of silver has not yet come.

Iokanaan to Salome in *Salome* (1894).

The image of the angel of death was used by John Bright in a speech in the House of Commons on February 23, 1855, while condemning the Crimean War; Herod's death, by the angel of the Lord, is depicted in Acts 12:23.

ANNUNCIATION

I sought this holy place,
And now with wondering eyes and heart I stand
Before this supreme mystery of Love:
Some kneeling girl with passionless pale face,
An angel with a lily in his hand,
And over both the white wings of a Dove.

"Ave Maria Plena Gratia," in *Irish Monthly* (July 1878), repr. in *Poems* (1997).

The title means "Hail Mary, full of grace," the first words of a Catholic prayer; the speaker in the poem is apparently gazing at a painting depicting the Annunciation, when the angel Gabriel informed Mary that she would conceive Jesus, the dove symbolizing the presence of the Holy Spirit.

APPEARANCE

Appearance is, in fact, a matter of effect merely, and it is with the effects of nature that you have to deal, not with the real condition of the object. What you, as painters, have to paint is not things as they are but things as they seem to be, not things as they are but things as they are not.

"Lecture to Art Students," of the Royal Academy (June 30, 1883), pub. in *Miscellanies*, 318.

To paint what you see is a good rule in art, but to see what is worth painting is better. See life under pictorial conditions. It is better to live in a city of changeable weather than in a city of lovely surroundings.

"Lecture to Art Students," of the Royal Academy (June 30, 1883), pub. in *Miscellanies*, 319.

$\mathcal{A}$RCHAEOLOGY

I can understand archaeology being attacked on the ground of its excessive realism, but to attack it as pedantic seems to be very much beside the mark. However, to attack it for any reason is foolish; one might just as well speak disrespectfully of the equator.

"The Truth of Masks," in *Intentions* (1891), repr. in Ellmann, 420.

Wilde had approved of archaeological research for historical accuracy in stage costumes and sets.

$\mathcal{A}$RGUMENTS

It is only the intellectually lost who ever argue.

Lord Henry in *Dorian Gray*, ch. 1.

I dislike arguments of any kind. They are always vulgar, and often convincing.

Lady Bracknell in *Earnest*, act 3.

$\mathcal{A}$RISTOCRACY

Thirty-five is a very attractive age. London society is full of women of the very highest birth who have, of their own free choice, remained thirty-five for years.

Lady Bracknell in *Earnest*, act 3.

$\mathcal{A}$RNOLD, MATTHEW

I have only now, too late perhaps, found out how all art requires solitude as its companion, only now indeed know the splendid difficulty of this great art [poetry] in which you are a master illustrious and supreme.

Letters, 78.

Written in the summer of 1881.

*A*RT *AND ARTISTS*

Art, in a word, must not content itself simply with holding the mirror up to nature, for it is a re-creation more than a reflection, and not a repetition but rather a new song.

"Art at Willis's Rooms," *Sunday Times* (December 25, 1887), repr. in *Miscellanies*, 91.

All art is immoral. . . . For emotion for the sake of emotion is the aim of art, and emotion for the sake of action is the aim of life, and of that practical organization of life that we call society. Society . . . exists simply for the concentration of human energy, and in order to ensure its own continuance and healthy stability, it demands, and no doubt rightly demands, of each of its citizens that he should contribute some form of productive labour to the common weal. . . .

Gilbert in "The Critic as Artist," pt. 2, in *Intentions* (1891), repr. in Ellmann, 380.

All artistic creation is absolutely subjective. The very landscape that Corot looked at was, as he said himself, but a mood of his own mind.

Gilbert in "The Critic as Artist," pt. 2, in *Intentions* (1891), repr. in Ellmann, 389.

It is a strange thing, this transference of emotion. We sicken with the same maladies as the poets, and the singer lends us his pain. Dead lips have their message for us, and hearts that have fallen to dust can communicate their joy.

Gilbert in "The Critic as Artist," pt. 2, in *Intentions* (1891), repr. in Ellmann, 379.

So far from its being true that the artist is the best judge of art, a really great artist can never judge of other people's work at all, and can hardly, in fact, judge of his own. That very concentration of vision that makes a man an artist, limits by its sheer intensity his faculty of fine appreciation. The energy of creation hurries him blindly on to his own goal.

Gilbert in "The Critic as Artist," pt. 2, in *Intentions* (1891), repr. in Ellmann, 400.

The sorrow with which Art fills us both purifies and initiates, if I may quote once more from the great art-critic of the Greeks. It is through Art, and through Art only, that we can realize our perfection; through Art, and through Art only, that we can shield ourselves from the sordid perils of actual existence.

Gilbert in "The Critic as Artist," pt. 2, in *Intentions* (1891), repr. in Ellmann, 380.

The "great art-critic" is, of course, Aristotle, whose *Treatise on Poetry* (or, the *Poetics*) Wilde cites in his writings.

The statue is concentrated to one moment of perfection. The image stained upon the canvas possesses no spiritual element of growth or change. If they know nothing of death, it is because they know little of life, for the secrets of life and death belong to those, and those only, whom the sequence of time affects. . . .

Gilbert in "The Critic as Artist," pt. 1, in *Intentions* (1891), repr. in Ellmann, 363.

The aim of art is simply to create a mood. Is such a mode of life unpractical? Ah! it is not so easy to be unpractical as the ignorant Philistine imagines. It were well for England if it were so. There is no country in the world so much in need of unpractical people as this country of ours.

Gilbert in "The Critic as Artist," pt. 2, in *Intentions* (1891), repr. in Ellmann, 385.

All bad art comes from returning to Life and Nature, and elevating them into ideals. Life and Nature may sometimes be used as part of Art's rough material, but before they are of any real service to art they must be translated into artistic conventions.

Vivian in "The Decay of Lying," in *Intentions* (1891), repr. in Ellmann, 319.

Art finds her own perfection within, and not outside of, herself. She is not to be judged by any external standard of resemblance. She is a veil, rather than a mirror. She has flowers that no forests know of, birds that no woodland possesses. She makes and unmakes many worlds, and can draw the moon from heaven with a scarlet thread.

Vivian in "The Decay of Lying," in *Intentions* (1891), repr. in Ellmann, 306.

Art is our spirited protest, our gallant attempt to teach Nature her proper place.

Vivian in "The Decay of Lying," in *Intentions* (1891), repr. in Ellmann, 291.

Art never expresses anything but itself. This is the principle of my new aesthetics; and it is this, more than that vital connection between form and substance, on which Mr. Pater dwells, that makes music the type of all the arts.

Vivian in "The Decay of Lying," in *Intentions* (1891), repr. in Ellmann, 313-14.

Vivian's "new aesthetics" had already been written about for more than fifty years—first in France as *l'art pour l'art*, then in England as "art for art's sake"; the allusion to Walter Pater refers to his essay "The School of Giorgione," in *FR* (October 1877), repr. in *The Renaissance* (3rd ed., 1888): "All art constantly aspires towards the condition of music."

Art takes life as part of her rough material, recreates it, and refashions it in fresh forms, is absolutely indifferent to fact, invents, imagines, dreams, and keeps between herself and reality the impenetrable barrier of beautiful style, of decorative or ideal treatment.

Vivian in "The Decay of Lying," in *Intentions* (1891), repr. in Ellmann, 301.

Art, breaking from the prison-house of realism, will run to greet [the liar], and will kiss his false, beautiful lips, knowing that he alone is in possession of the great secret of all her manifestations, the secret that Truth is entirely and absolutely a matter of style; while Life—poor, probable, uninteresting human life— . . . will follow meekly after him, and try to produce, in her own simple and untutored way, some of the marvels of which he talks.

Vivian in "The Decay of Lying," in *Intentions* (1891), repr. in Ellmann, 305.

Enjoy Nature! I am glad to say that I have entirely lost that faculty. People tell us that Art makes us love Nature more than we loved her before; that it reveals secrets to us. . . . My own experience is that the more we study Art, the less we care for Nature.

Vivian in "The Decay of Lying," in *Intentions* (1891), repr. in Ellmann, 290.

No great artist ever sees things as they are. If he did, he would cease to be an artist. . . . Now, do you really imagine that the Japanese people, as they are presented to us in art, have any existence? If you do, you have never understood Japanese art at all. The Japanese people are the deliberate self-conscious creation of certain individual artists.

Vivian in "The Decay of Lying," in *Intentions* (1891), repr. in Ellmann, 315.

[The novelist] is to be found at the Librairie Nationale, or at the British Museum, shamelessly reading up his subject. He has not even the courage of other people's ideas, but insists on going directly to life for everything, and ultimately, between encyclopaedias and personal experience, he comes to the ground . . . having acquired an amount of useful information from which never, even in his most meditative moments, can he thoroughly free himself.

Vivian in "The Decay of Lying," in *Intentions* (1891), repr. in Ellmann, 293-94.
Here, Wilde condemns Zola's Naturalism.

What Art really reveals to us is Nature's lack of design, her curious crudities, her extraordinary monotony, her absolutely unfinished condition. Nature had good intentions, of course, but, as Aristotle once said, she cannot carry them out.

> Vivian in "The Decay of Lying," in *Intentions* (1891), repr. in Ellmann, 290-91.

Art culture will do more to train children to be kind to animals and all living things than all our harrowing moral tales, for when he sees how lovely the little leaping squirrel is on the beaten brass or the bird arrested in flight on carven marble, he will not throw the customary stone.

> "The Decorative Arts," in O'Brien, 164.

If you teach a boy art, the beauty of form and colour will find its way into his heart, and he will love nature more; for there is no better way to learn to love nature than to understand art—it dignifies every flower of the field.

> "The Decorative Arts," in O'Brien, 164.

Let it be for you to create an art that is made with the hands of the people, for the joy of the people, too, an art that will be an expression of your delight in life. There is nothing in common life too mean, in common things too trivial to be ennobled by your touch; nothing in life that art cannot sanctify.

> "The Decorative Arts," in O'Brien, 165; the last sentence in the passage reappears in "The House Beautiful," in O'Brien, 181.

All art is at once surface and symbol. Those who go beneath the surface do so at their peril. Those who read the symbol do so at their peril.

> *Dorian Gray*, Preface.
>
> A similar view is expressed by Herod in *Salome* (1894): "It is not wise to find symbols in everything that one sees. It makes life too full of terrors."

All art is quite useless.

> *Dorian Gray*, Preface.
>
> Meaning that art cannot (or should not) be used to advance political, religious, or social agendas.

DUCHESS OF MONMOUTH: What of Art?
LORD HENRY: It is a malady.
DUCHESS: Love?
LORD HENRY: An illusion.

DUCHESS: Religion?
LORD HENRY: The fashionable substitute for Belief.

> Dorian Gray, ch. 17.

Good artists exist simply in what they make, and consequently are perfectly uninteresting in what they are. A great poet, a really great poet, is the most unpoetical of all creatures. But inferior poets are absolutely fascinating. The worse their rhymes are, the more picturesque they look.

> Lord Henry in Dorian Gray, ch. 4.

It often seems to me that art conceals the artist far more completely than it ever reveals him.

> Basil Hallward in Dorian Gray, ch. 9, echoed from the Preface.

No artist has ethical sympathies. An ethical sympathy in an artist is an unpardonable mannerism of style.

> Dorian Gray, Preface.

The only artists I have ever known, who are personally delightful, are bad artists. . . . The mere fact of having published a book of second-rate sonnets makes a man quite irresistible. He lives the poetry that he cannot write. The others write the poetry that they dare not realize.

> Lord Henry in Dorian Gray, ch. 4.

To reveal art and conceal the artist is art's aim.

> Dorian Gray, Preface.

We live in an age when men treat art as if it were meant to be a form of autobiography. We have lost the abstract sense of beauty.

> Basil Hallward in Dorian Gray, ch. 1.

We must always remember that art has only one sentence to utter: there is for her only one high law, the law of form or harmony. . . .

> "English Renaissance," pub. in Miscellanies, 244.

Art is what makes the life of each citizen a sacrament and not a speculation, art is what makes the life of the whole race immortal.

> "English Renaissance," pub. in Miscellanies, 268.

Art never harms itself by keeping aloof from the social problems of the day: rather, by so doing, it more completely realises for us that which we desire.

"English Renaissance," pub. in *Miscellanies*, 256.

A basic principle of Aestheticism.

Love art for its own sake, and then all things that you need will be added to you. This devotion to beauty and to the creation of beautiful things is the test of all great civilised nations. . . .

"English Renaissance," pub. in *Miscellanies*, 268.

Art for art's sake: a basic principle of Aestheticism.

The good we get from art is not what we learn from it; it is what we become through it. Its real influence will be in giving the mind that enthusiasm which is the secret of Hellenism, accustoming it to demand from art all that art can do in rearranging the facts of common life for us . . . he who does not love art in all things does not love it at all, and he who does not need art in all things does not need it at all.

"English Renaissance," pub. in *Miscellanies*, 273.

The artist is indeed the child of his own age, but the present will not be to him a whit more real than the past; for, like the philosopher of the Platonic vision, the poet is the spectator of all time and of all existence. For him no form is obsolete, no subject out of date. . . .

"English Renaissance," pub. in *Miscellanies*, 256.

The recognition of a separate realm for the artist, a consciousness of the absolute difference between the world of art and the world of real fact, between classic grace and absolute reality, forms not merely the essential element of any aesthetic charm but is the characteristic of all great imaginative work and of all great eras of artistic creation. . . .

"English Renaissance," pub. in *Miscellanies*, 256.

Whatever spiritual message an artist brings to his aid is a matter for his own soul. . . . But for warrant of its truth such message must have the flame of eloquence in the lips that speak it, splendour and glory in the vision that is its witness, being justified by one thing only—the flawless beauty and perfect form of its expression. . . .

"English Renaissance," pub. in *Miscellanies*, 259-60.

A basic principle of Aestheticism.

Sincerity and constancy will the artist, indeed, have always; but sincerity in art is merely that plastic perfection of execution without which a poem or a painting, however noble its sentiment or human its origin, is but wasted and unreal work, and the constancy of the artist cannot be to any definite rule or system of living, but to that principle of beauty only through which the inconstant shadows of his life are in their most fleeting moment arrested and made permanent.

"L'Envoi," in Rennell Rodd's *Rose Leaf and Apple Leaf* (Philadelphia, 1882), repr. in *Miscellanies*, 38.

Art is the only serious thing in the world. And the artist is the only person who is never serious.

"A Few Maxims," repr. in *Letters*, 870.

Nothing that is made is too trivial or too poor for art to ennoble, for genius can glorify stone, metal, and wood by the manner in which these simple materials are fashioned and shaped.

"The House Beautiful," in O'Brien, 165.

Today more than ever the artist and a love of the beautiful are needed to temper and counteract the sordid materialism of the age. In an age when science has undertaken to declaim against the soul and spiritual nature of man, and when commerce is ruining beautiful rivers and magnificent woodlands and the glorious skies in its greed for gain, the artist comes forward as a priest and prophet of nature to protest. . . .

"The House Beautiful," pub. in O'Brien, 180-81.

A picture is finished when all traces of work, and of the means employed to bring about the result, have disappeared.

"Lecture to Art Students," of the Royal Academy (June 30, 1883), pub. in *Miscellanies*, 320-21.

The sign of a Philistine age is the cry of immorality against art, and this cry was raised by the Athenian people against every great poet and thinker of their day—Aeschylus, Euripides, Socrates.

"Lecture to Art Students," of the Royal Academy (June 30, 1883), pub. in *Miscellanies*, 315.

To me the most inartistic thing in this age of ours is not the indifference of the public to beautiful things, but the indifference of the artist to the things that are called ugly. For, to the real artist, nothing is beautiful or ugly in itself at all. With the facts of the object he has nothing to do, but with its appearance only, and appearance is a matter of light and shade, of masses, of position, and of value.

"Lecture to Art Students," of the Royal Academy (June 30, 1883), pub. in *Miscellanies*, 318.

What would you say of a dramatist who would take nobody but virtuous people as characters in his play? Would you not say he was missing half of life? Well, of the young artist who paints nothing but beautiful things, I say he misses one half of the world.

"Lecture to Art Students," of the Royal Academy (June 30, 1883), pub. in *Miscellanies*, 319.

The sphere of art and the sphere of ethics are absolutely distinct and separate.

Letters, 257.
Written to the Editor, *St. James's Gazette*, on June 25, 1890, in defense of *Dorian Gray*.

Art is useless because its aim is simply to create a mood. It is not meant to instruct, or to influence action in any way. It is superbly sterile, and the note of its pleasure is sterility. If the contemplation of a work of art is followed by activity of any kind, the work is either of a very second-rate order, or the spectator has failed to realise the complete artistic impression.

Letters, 292.
Written to R. Clegg (unidentified) in Apr. 1891.

Art only begins where Imitation ends.

Letters, 489.
Written to Alfred Douglas in early 1897 from Reading Prison, partly pub. as *De Profundis* (1905).

I treated Art as the supreme reality, and life as a mere mode of fiction: I awoke the imagination of my century so that it created myth and legend around me: I summed up all systems in a phrase, and all existence in an epigram.

Letters, 466.
Written to Alfred Douglas in early 1897 from Reading Prison, partly pub. as *De Profundis* (1905).

I was a man who stood in symbolic relations to the art and culture of my age. . . . The gods had given me almost everything. I had genius, a distinguished name, high social position, brilliancy, intellectual daring: I made art a philosophy, and philosophy an art: I altered the minds of men and the colours of things: there was nothing I said or did that did not make people wonder. . . .

Letters, 466.

Written to Alfred Douglas in early 1897 from Reading Prison, partly pub. as *De Profundis* (1905).

In an age like this when Slander, and Ridicule, and Envy walk quite unashamed among us, and when any attempt to produce serious beautiful work is greeted with a very tornado of lies and evil-speaking, it is a wonderful joy, a wonderful spur for ambition and work, to receive any such encouragement and appreciation as your letter brought me. . . .

Letters, 79.

Written to the novelist Violet Hunt in July 1881.

In art good intentions are not of the smallest value. All bad art is the result of good intentions.

Letters, 495.

Written to Alfred Douglas in early 1897 from Reading Prison, partly pub. as *De Profundis* (1905).

It is a great fight in this commercial age to plead the cause of Art. Still the principles which I represent are so broad, so grand, so noble that I have no fear for the future.

Letters, 128.

Written to the actress Mary Anderson in October 1882.

No artist recognises any standard of beauty but that which is suggested by his own temperament. The artist seeks to realise in a certain material his immaterial idea of beauty, and thus to transform an idea into an ideal.

Letters, 302.

Written to the Editor, *PMG,* in December 1891.

Sometimes I think that the artistic life is a long and lovely suicide, and am not sorry that it is so.

Letters, 185.

Written to H. C. Marillier, an acquaintance, in early 1886.

The function of the artist is to invent, not chronicle.

Letters, 259.

Written to the Editor, *St. James's Gazette* on June 26, 1890 in defense of *Dorian Gray*.

The aim of art is no more to give pleasure than to give pain. The aim of art is to be art. As I said once before, the work of art is to dominate the spectator—the spectator is not to dominate art.

Quoted in: "Mr Oscar Wilde on Mr Oscar Wilde: An Interview," *St. James's Gazette* (January 18, 1895), unsigned but probably written by Robert Ross and Wilde; repr. in Mikahil 1:247.

Ross asked Wilde whether it was the duty of the dramatist to please the public.

[The nightingale] has form . . . but has she got feeling? I am afraid not. In fact, she is like most artists; she is all style, without any sincerity. She would not sacrifice herself for others. She thinks merely of music, and everybody knows that the arts are selfish.

The Student in "The Nightingale and the Rose," pub. in *The Happy Prince*.

Wilde's ironic view of the nightingale as artist.

The fact of a man being a poisoner is nothing against his prose. The domestic virtues are not the true basis of art, though they serve as an excellent advertisement for second-rate artists.

"Pen, Pencil, and Poison," in *Intentions* (1891), repr. in Ellmann, 339.

The poisoner alluded to is Thomas Griffiths Wainewright.

A really well-made buttonhole is the only link between Art and Nature.

"Phrases and Philosophies," repr. in Ellmann, 433.

Only the great masters of style ever succeed in being obscure.

"Phrases and Philosophies," repr. in Ellmann, 434.

To love oneself is the beginning of a life-long romance.

"Phrases and Philosophies," repr. in Ellmann, 434.

Art is not to be taught in Academies. It is what one looks at, not what one listens to, that makes the artist. The real schools should be the streets.

"The Relation of Dress to Art: A Note in Black and White on Mr. Whistler's Lecture," *PMG* (February 28, 1885), repr. in Ellmann, 19.

On Whistler's "Ten O'Clock" lecture, delivered on February 20, 1885.

An unhealthy work of art . . . is a work whose style is obvious, old-fashioned, and common, and whose subject is deliberately chosen, not because the artist has any pleasure in it, but because he thinks that the public will pay him for it. In fact, the popular novel that the public calls healthy is always a thoroughly unhealthy production; and what the public call an unhealthy novel is always a beautiful and healthy work of art.

"The Soul of Man," repr. in Ellmann, 275.

Art is the most intense mode of Individualism that the world has known. I am inclined to say that it is the only real mode of Individualism that the world has known.

"The Soul of Man," repr. in Ellmann, 270.

Art is Individualism, and Individualism is a disturbing and disintegrating force. Therein lies its immense value. For what it seeks to disturb is monotony of type, slavery of custom, tyranny of habit, and the reduction of man to the level of a machine.

"The Soul of Man," repr. in Ellmann, 272.

If a man approaches a work of art with any desire to exercise authority over it and the artist, he approaches it in such a spirit that he cannot receive any artistic impression from it at all. *The work of art is to dominate the spectator: the spectator is not to dominate the work of art.* The spectator is to be receptive. He is to be the violin on which the master is to play.

"The Soul of Man," repr. in Ellmann, 279.

Now Art should never try to be popular. The public should try to make itself artistic.

"The Soul of Man," repr. in Ellmann, 271.

The artist is never morbid. He expresses everything. He stands outside his subject, and through its medium produces incomparable and artistic effects. To call an artist morbid because he deals with morbidity as his subject-matter is as silly as if one called Shakespeare mad because he wrote *King Lear.*

"The Soul of Man," repr. in Ellmann, 274.

The first two sentences are echoed in *Dorian Gray,* Preface.

The artist's view of life is the only possible one and should be applied to everything, most of all to religion and morality. Cavaliers and Puritans are interesting for their costumes and not for their convictions. . . .

Quoted in: Harris, ch. 6.

Most women are so artificial that they have no sense of art. Most men are so natural that they have no sense of beauty.

Quoted in: Small, 127.

To become a work of art is the object of living.

Quoted in: Small, 127.

$\mathcal{A}$TONEMENT

He atones for being occasionally somewhat over-dressed, by being always absolutely over-educated.

Lord Henry in *Dorian Gray*, ch. 15; the aphorism, in slightly different form, reappears in "Phrases and Philosophies" and in Algernon's remark about himself in *Earnest*, act 2: "If I am occasionally a little over-dressed, I make up for it by being always immensely over-educated."

Lord Henry commenting on Lord Grotrian.

$\mathcal{A}$USTRALIA

CECILY: Uncle Jack is sending you to Australia.
ALGERNON: Australia! I'd sooner die.
CECILY: Well, he said at dinner on Wednesday night, that you would have to choose between this world, the next world, and Australia.
ALGERNON: Oh, well! The accounts I have received of Australia and the next world are not particularly encouraging. This world is good enough for me. . . .

Earnest, act 2.

Algernon Moncrieff is pretending to be Jack Worthing's wicked brother, Ernest.

When I look at the map and see what an awfully ugly-looking country Australia is, I feel as if I want to go there to see if it cannot be changed into a more beautiful form.

Quoted in: Lewis and Smith, 420.

In an interview, in October 1882, with a *New York Herald* reporter.

$\mathcal{A}$UTHORITY

With authority, punishment will pass away. This will be a great gain—a gain, in fact, of incalculable value. As one reads history . . . one is absolutely sickened, not by the crimes that the wicked have committed, but by the punishments that the good have inflicted; *and a community is infinitely more brutalised by the habitual employment of punishment, than it is by the occasional occurrence of crime.*

"The Soul of Man," repr. in Ellmann, 267.

$\mathcal{A}$UTOBIOGRAPHY

I dislike modern memoirs. They are generally written by people who have either entirely lost their memories, or have never done anything worth remembering; which, however, is, no doubt, the true explanation of their popularity, as the English public always feels perfectly at its ease when a mediocrity is talking to it.

Ernest in "The Critic as Artist," pt. 1, in *Intentions* (1891), repr. in Ellmann, 341.

$\mathcal{B}$ACHELORS

ALGERNON: Why is it that at a bachelor's establishment the servants
   invariably drink the champagne? I ask merely for information.
LANE: I attribute it to the superior quality of the wine, sir. I have often
   observed that in married households the champagne is rarely of a first-
   rate brand.
ALGERNON: Good heavens! Is marriage so demoralizing as that?

Earnest, act 1.

MISS PRISM: You do not seem to realize, dear Doctor, that by persistently
   remaining single, a man converts himself into a permanent public

temptation. Men should be more careful; this very celibacy leads weaker vessels astray.

CHASUBLE: But is a man not equally attractive when married?

MISS PRISM: No married man is ever attractive except to his wife.

Earnest, act 2.

ℬANKRUPTCY

Most people become bankrupt through having invested too heavily in the prose of life. To have ruined one's self over poetry is an honour.

Lord Henry in *Dorian Gray*, ch. 4.

Commenting on the East End theatre manager's five bankruptcies entirely due to productions of Shakespeare's plays.

ℬEAUTY

Behind every exquisite thing that existed, there was something tragic.

Dorian Gray, ch. 3.

He grew more and more enamoured of his own beauty, more and more interested in the corruption of his own soul. He would examine with minute care, and sometimes with a monstrous and terrible delight, the hideous lines that seared the wrinking forehead or crawled around the heavy sensual mouth, wondering sometimes which were the more horrible, the signs of sin or the signs of age.

Dorian Gray, ch. 11.

Dorian's obsession with his disintegrating portrait.

Spirit of Beauty! tarry still a-while,
They are not dead, thine ancient votaries,
Some few there are to whom thy radiant smile
 Is better than a thousand victories. . . .

"The Garden of Eros," lines 103-06, in *Poems* (1881), repr. in *Poems* (1997).

The phrase "Spirit of Beauty" is from Shelley's "Hymn to Intellectual Beauty" (1817); the passage was inscribed in Wilde's library in Tite Street.

How strange to live in a land where the worship of beauty and the passion of love are considered infamous. I hate England: it is only bearable to me because you are here.

> *Letters*, 377.
> Written to Alfred Douglas in November 1894.

A fresh mode of Beauty is absolutely distasteful to [the public], and whenever it appears they get so angry and bewildered that they always use two stupid expressions—one is that the work of art is grossly unintelligible; the other, that the work of art is grossly immoral.

> "The Soul of Man," repr. in Ellmann, 273.

MRS. ALLONBY: Lord Illingworth told me this morning that there was an orchid [in the conservatory] as beautiful as the seven deadly sins.
LADY HUNSTANTON: My dear, I hope there is nothing of the kind. I will certainly speak to the gardener.

> *A Woman*, act 1.

BEERBOHM, MAX

The gods bestowed on Max the gift of perpetual old age.

> Quoted in: Vincent O'Sullivan, *Aspects of Wilde* (New York, 1936), 68.

When you are alone with him, Sphinx, does he take off his face and reveal his mask?

> Quoted in: "Reminiscences" by Ada Leverson, repr. in Wyndham, 119.
> "Sphinx" was Wilde's name for the satirist and novelist Leverson.

BEHAVIOR

One should never do anything that one cannot talk about after dinner.

> Lord Henry in *Dorian Gray*, ch. 19.

LADY BRACKNELL: I hope you are behaving very well.
ALGERNON: I'm feeling very well, Aunt Augusta.

LADY BRACKNELL: That's not quite the same thing. In fact the two things rarely go together.

Earnest, act 1.

BELIEF

I can believe anything, provided that it is quite incredible.

Lord Henry in *Dorian Gray*, ch. 1.

I am sad because half the world does not believe in God, and the other half does not believe in me.

Quoted in: Jacques Daurelle's "An English Poet in Paris," *Echo de Paris* (December 6, 1891), repr. in Mikhail 1:170.

BOOKS

The books that the world calls immoral are books that show the world its own shame. That is all.

Lord Henry in *Dorian Gray*, ch. 19.

There is no such thing as a moral or an immoral book. Books are well written, or badly written. That is all.

Dorian Gray, Preface.

In old days books were written by men of letters and read by the public. Nowadays books are written by the public and read by nobody.

"A Few Maxims," repr. in *Letters*, 869.

BOREDOM

Bored by the tedious and improving conversation of those who have neither the wit to exaggerate nor the genius to romance, tired of the intelligent person whose reminiscences are always based upon memory, whose statements are invariably limited by probability, who is at any time liable to be corroborated by the merest Philistine who happens to be present, Society sooner or later must return to its lost leader, the cultured and fascinating liar.

Vivian in "The Decay of Lying," in *Intentions* (1891), repr. in Ellmann, 305.

BRAIN, THE

It is in the brain, and the brain only, that the great sins of the world take place. . . .

Lord Henry in *Dorian Gray*, ch. 2.

BRIBERY

My dear Sir Robert, you are a man of the world, and you have your price, I suppose. Everybody has nowadays. The drawback is that most people are so dreadfully expensive.

Mrs. Cheveley in *Husband*, act 1.

BROTHERS

I don't care for brothers. My elder brother won't die, and my younger brothers seem never to do anything else.

Basil Hallward in *Dorian Gray*, ch. 1.

When one is placed in the position of guardian, one has to adopt a very high moral tone on all subjects. It's one's duty to do so. And as a high moral tone can hardly be said to conduce very much to either one's health or one's happiness, in order to get up to town I have always pretended to have a younger brother of the name of Ernest, who lives in the Albany, and gets into the most dreadful scrapes.

Jack Worthing in *Earnest*, act 1.

BROWNING, ELIZABETH BARRETT

Her view of the poet's mission . . . was to utter Divine oracles, to be at once inspired prophet and holy priest; and as such we may, I think, without exaggeration, conceive her. She was a Sibyl delivering a message to the world, sometimes through stammering lips, and once at least with blinded eyes, yet always with the true fire and fervour of lofty and unshaken faith, always with the great raptures of a spiritual nature, the high ardours of an impassioned soul.

"English Poetesses," in the *Queen* (December 8, 1888), repr. in Ellmann, 104.

England has given to the world one great poetess—Elizabeth Barrett Browning. By her side Mr. Swinburne would place Miss Christina Rossetti, whose New Year hymn he describes as so much the noblest of sacred poems in our language, that there is none which comes near it enough to stand second.

"English Poetesses," in the *Queen* (December 8, 1888), repr. in Ellmann, 101.

Of all the women of history, Mrs. Browning is the only one that we could name in any possible or remote conjunction with Sappho. Sappho was undoubtedly a far more flawless and perfect artist. She stirred the whole antique world more than Mrs. Browning ever stirred our modern age. Never had Love such a singer.

"English Poetesses," in the *Queen* (December 8, 1888), repr. in Ellmann, 102.

BROWNING, ROBERT

And as what will he be remembered? As a poet? Ah, not as a poet! He will be remembered as a writer of fiction, as the most supreme writer of fiction, it may be, that we have ever had. His sense of dramatic situation was unrivalled, and, if he could not answer his own problems, he could at least put problems forth, and what more should an artist do?

Gilbert in "The Critic as Artist," pt. 1, in *Intentions* (1891), repr. in Ellmann, 346.

Considered from the point of view of a creator of character he ranks next to him who made Hamlet. Had he been articulate, he might have sat beside him.

Gilbert in "The Critic as Artist," pt. 1, in *Intentions* (1891), repr. in Ellmann, 346.

Taken as whole, the man was great. He did not belong to the Olympians, and had all the incompleteness of the Titan. He did not survey, and it was but rarely that he could sing. His work is marred by struggle, violence and effort, and he passed not from emotion to form, but from thought to chaos. Still, he was great.

Gilbert in "The Critic as Artist," pt. 1, in *Intentions* (1891), repr. in Ellmann, 344.

The only man who can touch the hem of his garment is George Meredith. Meredith is a prose Browning, and so is Browning. He used poetry as medium for writing in prose.

Gilbert in "The Critic as Artist," pt. 1, in *Intentions* (1891), repr. in Ellmann, 346.

Though he turned language into ignoble clay, he made from it men and women that live. He is the most Shakespearian creature since Shakespeare. If Shakespeare could sing with myriad lips, Browning could stammer through a thousand mouths.

Gilbert in "The Critic as Artist," pt. 1, in *Intentions* (1891), repr. in Ellmann, 345.

Where one had hoped that Browning was a mystic, they have sought to show that he was simply inarticulate. Where one had fancied that he had something to conceal, they have proved that he had but little to reveal.

Gilbert in "The Critic as Artist," pt. 1, in *Intentions* (1891), repr. in Ellmann, 344.

"They" refers to members of the Browning Society.

Is it possible that Mr. Browning can see nothing in the world around him to induce him to make an earnest endeavour to help the people out of their difficulties and to make their duty plain? He may be a man of genius so sublime that the language of the common people is inadequate to clothe his thoughts, but his right to the title of poet is not so clear as that of the humblest writer of doggerel lines in the poets' corner of a provincial newspaper. . . .

"The Poets and the People," in *PMG* (February 17, 1887), repr. in Ellmann, 45.

Let any sensible man outside the Browning Society dip into the mysterious volume of literary hocus-pocus that has recently been so solemnly reviewed, and see whether he can find a single passage likely to stir the pulses of any man or woman, or create a desire to lead a higher, a holier, and a more useful life in the breast of the indifferent average citizen.

"The Poets and the People," in *PMG* (February 17, 1887), repr. in Ellmann, 45.

The "mysterious volume" is Browning's *Parleyings with Certain People of Importance in their Day*.

The Roman despot who played the fiddle while his city was burning might plead the ignorance of himself and his time, but Mr. Browning is living in the nineteenth century, and has no such excuses for banging his intellectual tin kettle while a fourth part of his fellow-countrymen are struggling against poverty, and are weighed down by the gloomy outlook towards the future.

"The Poets and the People," in *PMG* (February 17, 1887), repr. in Ellmann, 44-45.

What shall be said of the conduct of one who in the eyes of many is esteemed the greatest of living poets? He, at the hour when his country requires inspiration and encouragement, prostitutes his intelligence to the production of a number of unwieldly lines that to the vast majority of Englishmen are unintelligible jargon.

"The Poets and the People," in *PMG* (February 17, 1887), repr. in Ellmann, 44.

The unnamed poet is Robert Browning.

$\mathcal{B}$URIAL

Poor Osgood! He is a great loss to us! However, I suppose they will bury him simultaneously in London and New York.

Quoted in: Richard Le Gallienne, *The Romantic '90s* (1926), 152.

On the occasion of the death of James R. Osgood, of the publishing firm of Osgood, McIlvaine and Co., Wilde's publisher, who habitually advertised that all their books were "published simultaneously in London and New York."

$\mathcal{B}$USINESS

I know, of course, how important it is not to keep a business engagement, if one wants to retain any sense of the beauty of life. . . .

Cecily Cardew in *Earnest*, act 2.

To me the life of the businessman who eats his breakfast early in the morning, catches a train for the city, stays there in the dingy, dusty atmosphere of the commercial world, and goes back to his house in the evening, and after supper to sleep, is worse than the life of the galley slave—his chains are golden instead of iron.

Quoted in: Lewis and Smith, 337.

From an interview with a reporter from the *Topeka Capital* in April 1882.

BYRON, LORD

Then rise supreme Athena argent-limbed!
And, if my lips be musicless, inspire
At least my life: was not thy glory hymned
By One who gave to thee his sword and lyre
Like Aeschylos at well-fought Marathon,
And died to show that Milton's England still could bear a son!

"Humanitad," lines 163-68, in *Poems* (1881), repr. in *Poems* (1997).

"One" is undoubtedly Lord Byron, who, in 1824, died while assisting the Greeks in their struggle against the Turks for independence; Aeschylus did not die in the battle of Marathon against the Persians.

And England, too, shall glory in her son,
Her warrior-poet, first in song and fight.
No longer now shall Slander's venomed spite
Crawl like a snake across his perfect name,
Or mar the lordly scutcheon of his fame.

Ravenna, lines 134-38 (Oxford, 1878), repr. in *Poems* (1997).

Lord Byron, an exile from England (because of rumors of incest), is here praised for his participation in the Greek war of independence from Turkey; like Dante, he, too, lived for a while in Ravenna.

Byron dwelt here in love and revelry
For two long years—a second Anthony,
Who of the world another Actium made!—
Yet suffered not his royal soul to fade....

Ravenna, lines 113-16 (Oxford, 1878), repr. in *Poems* (1997).

Mark Anthony, alienated from Rome because of his relationship with Cleopatra, was defeated in a confrontation with Octavian (later known as Augustus) at Actium in 31 BC.

Byron's personality ... was terribly wasted in its battle with the stupidity, and hypocrisy, and Philistinism of the English. Such battles do not always intensify strength: they often exaggerate weakness. Byron was never able to give us what he might have given us.

"The Soul of Man," repr. in Ellmann, 262.

CALIFORNIA

California is an Italy without its art. There are subjects for the artist, but it is universally true that the only scenery which inspires utterance is that which man feels himself the master of. The mountains of California are so gigantic that they are not favorable to art or poetry. There are good poets in England but none in Switzerland. There the mountains are too high. Art cannot add to nature.

Quoted in: Lewis and Smith, 306.

In an interview, in April 1882, with a *Denver Tribune* reporter.

CAMBRIDGE UNIVERSITY

I hope you are enjoying yourself at Cambridge—whatever people may say against Cambridge, it is certainly the best preparatory school for Oxford that I know.

Undated letter (ca. 1888) to Robert Ross, pub. in Small, 45.

CARICATURE

As I look about me, I am impelled for the first time to breathe a fervent prayer, "Save me from my disciples."

Quoted in: Lewis and Smith, 125.

Wilde, about to lecture in Boston in January 1882, had been confronted by a troop of Harvard students, who, aesthetically dressed to resemble him, took front-row seats.

This is one of the compliments that mediocrity pays to those who are not mediocre.

Quoted in: "Oscar Wilde Sees 'Patience,'" in the *New York Daily Tribune* (January 6, 1882) and variously quoted with variations, as in "Caricature is the tribute which mediocrity pays to genius" (quoted in: Lewis and Smith, 55).

Wilde allegedly uttered his remark during a performance of Gilbert and Sullivan's *Patience*, which many believed satirized him.

CELLINI, BENVENUTO

They are miners—men working in metals, so I lectured them on the Ethics of Art. I read them passages from the autobiography of Benvenuto Cellini and they seemed much delighted. I was reproved by my hearers for not having brought him with me. I explained that he had been dead for some little time which elicted the enquiry "Who shot him?"

Impressions of America, ed. Stuart Mason (Sunderland, 1906), repr. in Ellmann, 9-10.

Wilde, on his lecture tour in 1882, had reached Leadville, Colorado.

CELTIC POETRY

The influence of Celtic poetry was not merely the primary basis of Irish politics, the keystone of Irish liberty, for to it—to the Celtic imagination—we owe nearly all the great beauties of modern literature. . . .

Quoted in: Robert D. Pepper, ed., *Irish Poets and Poetry of the Nineteenth Century* (San Francisco, 1972), 28.

A report of Wilde's lecture in the *San Francisco Chronicle* (April 6, 1882).

CEMETERIES

Ah! sweet indeed to rest within the womb
Of Earth, great mother of eternal sleep,
But sweeter far for thee a restless tomb
In the blue cavern of an echoing deep. . . .

"The Grave of Shelley," in *Poems* (1881), repr. in *Poems* (1997).

Wilde had visited Shelley's grave in the Protestant Cemetery in Rome in the spring of 1877; the quotation alludes to Shelley's death by drowning.

CERTAINTY

The things one feels absolutely certain about are never true. That is the fatality of faith, and the lesson of romance.

Lord Henry in *Dorian Gray*, ch. 19.

CHAMPAGNE

CARSON: Do you drink champagne yourself?
WILDE: Yes. Iced champagne is a favourite drink of mine—strongly against my doctor's orders.

CARSON: Never mind your doctor's orders, sir!
WILDE: I never do.

Quoted in: Hyde, 129.

The barrister Edward Carson questioning Wilde in the April 1895 libel trial involving the Marquess of Queensberry, who had charged that Wilde was "posing" as a sodomite.

CHANGE

I don't desire to change anything in England except the weather.

Lord Henry in *Dorian Gray*, ch. 3.

Day by day the old order of things changes, and new modes of thought pass over our world, and it may be that, before many years, talking will have taken the place of literature, and the personal screech silenced the music of impersonal utterance. Something of the dignity of the literary calling will probably be lost, and it is perhaps a dangerous thing for a country to be too eloquent. . . .

"Should Geniuses Meet?" *CSR* (May 4, 1887), repr. in Mason, 39-40.

CHAOS

Is this the end of all that primal force
Which, in its changes being still the same,
From eyeless Chaos cleft its upward course,
Through ravenous seas and whirling rocks and flame,
Till the suns met in heaven and began
Their cycles, and the morning stars sang, and the Word was Man!

"Humanitad," lines 427-32, in *Poems* (1881), repr. in *Poems* (1997).

Wilde transforms the biblical passage in John 1:1 ("In the beginning was the Word . . . and the Word was God") to glorify Man in his vision of the evolutionary development to divine humanity.

I am inclined to think that Chaos is a stronger evidence for an Intelligent
Creator than Kosmos: the view might be expanded.

Letters, 362.

Written to Alfred Douglas in August 1894.

CHARACTER

If a character in a play is life-like, if we recognise it as true to nature, we
have no right to insist on the author explaining its genesis to us. We must
accept it as it is: and in the hands of a good dramatist mere presentation
can take the place of analysis, and indeed is often a more dramatic method,
because a more direct one.

"Ben Jonson," in *PMG* (September 20, 1886), repr. in Ellmann, 35.

CHARITY

Charity, as even those of whose religion it makes a formal part have been
compelled to acknowledge, creates a multitude of evils.

Gilbert in "The Critic as Artist," pt. 1, in *Intentions* (1891), repr. in Ellmann, 360.

CHARM

All charming people, I fancy, are spoiled. It is the secret of their attraction.

Erskine, in *Mr. W. H.*, pt. 1, repr. in Ellmann, 156.

CHICAGO

It was not until I had seen the water-works at Chicago that I realised the
wonders of machinery; the rise and fall of the steel rods, the symmetrical

motion of the great wheels is the most beautifully rhythmic thing I have
ever seen.

Impressions of America, ed. Stuart Mason (Sunderland, 1906), repr. in Ellmann, 7.

CHILDREN

Consider how susceptible children are to the influence of beauty, for they
are easily impressed and are pretty much what their surroundings make
them. How can you expect them, then, to tell the truth if everything about
them is telling lies, like the paper in the hall declaring itself marble?

"The Decorative Arts," in O'Brien, 162.

Children begin by loving their parents; as they grow older they judge them;
sometimes they forgive them.

Dorian Gray, ch. 5; the passage is echoed by Mrs. Arbuthnot in *A Woman*, act 2, though "sometimes" is
replaced by "rarely, if ever."

CHOICES

There are moments when one has to choose between living one's own life,
fully, entirely, completely—or dragging out some false, shallow, degrading
existence that the world in its hypocrisy demands.

Lord Darlington in *Fan*, act 2.

CHOPIN, FRÉDÉRIC

After playing Chopin, I feel as if I had been weeping over sins that I had
never committed, and mourning over tragedies that were not my own.

Gilbert in "The Critic as Artist," pt. 1, in *Intentions* (1891), repr. in Ellmann, 343.

CHRIST

Above all, Christ is the most supreme of Individualists. Humility, like the artistic accepance of all experiences, is merely a mode of manifestation. It is man's soul that Christ is always looking for.

Letters, 479.
Written to Alfred Douglas in early 1897 from Reading Prison, partly pub. as *De Profundis* (1905).

One [article contemplated] will be on Christ as the Precursor of the Romantic Movement in Life, that lovely subject which was revealed to me when I found myself in the company of the same sort of people Christ liked, outcasts and beggars.

Letters, 581-582.
Written to Robert Ross in May 1897 from France; the article was never written.

Behold! the Lord hath come. The Son of Man is at hand. The centaurs have hidden themselves in the rivers, and the nymphs have left the rivers, and are lying beneath the leaves in the forests.

Iokanaan's voice from the cistern in *Salome* (1894).
The second sentence echoes Matthew 3:2.

When Jesus talks about the poor he simply means personalities, just as when he talks about the rich he simply means people who have not developed their personalities.

"The Soul of Man," repr. in Ellmann, 263.

CITIES

And then look at the depressing, monotonous appearance of any modern city, the sombre dress of men and women, the meaningless and barren architecture, the colourless and dreadful surroundings. Without a beautiful national life, not sculpture merely, but all the arts will die.

"Lecture to Art Students," of the Royal Academy (June 30, 1883), pub. in *Miscellanies*, 318.

CIVILIZATION

I am certain that, as civilization progresses and we become more highly organized, the elect spirits of each age, the critical and cultured spirits, will grow less and less interested in actual life, and *will seek to gain their impressions almost entirely from what Art has touched.*

> Gilbert in "The Critic as Artist," pt. 2, in *Intentions* (1891), repr. in Ellmann, 374-75.

The fact is, that civilization requires slaves. The Greeks were quite right there. Unless there are slaves to do the ugly, horrible, uninteresting work, culture and contemplation become almost impossible. Human slavery is wrong, insecure, and demoralizing. On mechanical slavery, on the slavery of the machine, the future of the world depends.

> "The Soul of Man," repr. in Ellmann, 269.

CLERGY

Don't you realize that missionaries are the divinely provided food for destitute and underfed cannibals? Whenever they are on the brink of starvation, Heaven, in its infinite mercy, sends them a nice plump missionary.

> Quoted in: Richard Le Gallienne, *The Romantic '90s* (1926), 144.
> Wilde's remark to his wife, Constance, at a dinner party.

CLEVERNESS

JACK: I am sick to death of cleverness. Everybody is clever nowadays. You can't go anywhere without meeting clever people. The thing has become an absolute public nuisance. I wish to goodness we had a few fools left.
ALGERNON: We have.
JACK: I should extremely like to meet them. What do they talk about?
ALGERNON: The fools? Oh! about the clever people, of course.
JACK: What fools!

> *Earnest*, act 1.

How clever you are, my dear! You never mean a single word you say.

Lady Hunstanton to Mrs. Allonby in *A Woman*, act 2.

COMMERCE

I do not say anything against commercial people, for it is not commerce that destroys art; Genoa was built by its traders, Florence by its bankers, and Venice, loveliest of them all, by her noble and honest merchants.

"The Decorative Arts," in O'Brien, 156.

COMMON SENSE

Nowadays most people die of a sort of creeping common sense, and discover when it is too late that the only things one never regrets are one's mistakes.

Lord Henry in *Dorian Gray*, ch. 3.

CONCEIT

Nowadays so many conceited people go about Society pretending to be good, that I think it shows rather a sweet and modest disposition to pretend to be bad.

Lord Darlington in *Fan*, act 1.

CONFESSION

There is a luxury in self-reproach. When we blame ourselves we feel that no one else has a right to blame us. It is the confession, not the priest, that gives us absolution.

Dorian Gray, ch. 8.

ALGERNON: Do you really keep a diary? I'd give anything to look at it.
  May I?
CECILY: Oh no. You see, it is simply a very young girl's record of her own
  thoughts and impressions, and consequently meant for publication.
  When it appears in volume form I hope you will order a copy.

  Earnest, act 2.

I never travel without my diary. One should always have something
sensational to read in the train.

  Cecily Cardew in *Earnest*, act 2.

CONSCIENCE

. . . As for conscience,
Conscience is but the name which cowardice
Fleeing from battle scrawls upon its shield.

  Duke of Padua in *Duchess*, act 1.

CONSISTENCY

I have always been of opinion that consistency is the last refuge of the
unimaginative. . . .

  "The Relation of Dress to Art: A Note in Black and White on Mr. Whistler's Lecture," *PMG* (February
  28, 1885), repr. in Ellmann, 18.
  On Whistler's "Ten O'Clock" lecture, delivered on February 20, 1885.

CONSOLATION

The only thing that can console one for being poor is extravagance. The
only thing that can console one for being rich is economy.

  "A Few Maxims," repr. in *Letters*, 870.

CONTEMPLATION

To do nothing at all is the most difficult thing in the world, the most difficult and the most intellectual. To Plato, with his passion for wisdom, this was the noblest form of energy. To Aristotle, with his passion for knowledge, this was the noblest form of energy also. It was to this that the passion for holiness led the saint and the mystic of mediaeval days.

Gilbert in "The Critic as Artist," pt. 2, in *Intentions* (1891), repr. in Ellmann, 381.

It is to do nothing that the elect exist. Action is limited and relative. Unlimited and absolute is the vision of him who sits at ease and watches, who walks in loneliness and dreams. But we who are born at the close of this wonderful age, are at once too cultured and too critical, too intellectually subtle and too curious of exquisite pleasures, to accept any speculations about life in exchange for life itself.

Gilbert in "The Critic as Artist," pt. 2, in *Intentions* (1891), repr. in Ellmann, 381.

Yes, Ernest, the contemplative life, the life that has for its aim not *doing* but *being*, and not *being* merely, but *becoming*—that is what the critical spirit can give us. The gods live thus: either brooding over their own perfection, as Aristotle tells us, or, as Epicurus fancied, watching with the calm eyes of the spectator the tragi-comedy of the world that they have made.

Gilbert in "The Critic as Artist," pt. 2, in *Intentions* (1891), repr. in Ellmann, 384.

The first sentence on doing and being echoes Pater's essay on Wordsworth in *Appreciations* (1899) and Wilde's "A Chinese Sage," a review of a book on Chuang Tsŭ in the *Speaker* (February 8, 1890), repr. in Ellmann, 222.

CONTRADICTION

The well-bred contradict other people. The wise contradict themselves.

"Phrases and Philosophies," repr. in Ellmann, 433.

CONVERSATION

Conversation should touch everything, but should concentrate itself on nothing.

Gilbert in "The Critic as Artist," pt. 2, in *Intentions* (1891), repr. in Ellmann, 372.

CONVERSION

Ah! it is so easy to convert others. It is so difficult to convert oneself. To arrive at what one really believes, one must speak through lips different from one's own. To know the truth one must imagine myriads of falsehoods.

> Gilbert in "The Critic as Artist," pt. 2, in *Intentions* (1891), repr. in Ellmann, 391.

COURAGE

Throughout the world, in all times and in all ages, there have been those who have had the courage to advocate opinions that were for the time abhorred by the public. But if those who hold those opinions have the courage to maintain and defend them, it is absolutely certain that in the end the truth will prevail.

> "The House Beautiful," in O'Brien, 181.

COURTSHIP

JACK: Well—may I propose to you now?
GWENDOLEN: I think it would be an admirable opportunity. And to spare you any possible disappointment, Mr. Worthing, I think it only fair to tell you quite frankly beforehand that I am fully determined to accept you.

> *Earnest*, act 1.

COWARDICE

I decided that it was nobler and more beautiful to stay. . . . I did not want to be called a coward or a deserter. A false name, a disguise, a hunted life, all that is not for me. . . .

> *Letters*, 398.
>
> Written to Alfred Douglas on May 20, 1895, before Wilde's second criminal trial, on why he did not flee from England.

CREATIVITY

Man is least himself when he talks in his own person. Give him a mask, and he will tell you the truth.

> Gilbert in "The Critic as Artist," pt. 2, in *Intentions* (1891), repr. in Ellmann, 389.

There has never been a creative age that has not been critical also. For it is the critical faculty that invents fresh forms. The tendency of creation is to repeat itself. It is to the critical instinct that we owe each new school that springs up, each new mould that art finds ready to its hand.

> Gilbert in "The Critic as Artist," pt. 1, in *Intentions* (1891), repr. in Ellmann, 357.

I have been correcting the proofs of my poems. In the morning, after hard work, I took a comma out of one sentence. . . . In the afternoon, I put it back again.

> Quoted: in Robert Sherard's *The Life of Oscar Wilde* (New York, 1906), ch. 12.

CREDITORS

London is very dangerous: writters come out at night and writ one, the roaring of creditors towards dawn is frightful, and solicitors are getting rabies and biting people.

> *Letters*, 354.
> Written to Alfred Douglas in Apr. 1894; "writters" are those who serve writs, written commands issued by the courts.

CRIME

All crime is vulgar, just as all vulgarity is crime.

> Lord Henry in *Dorian Gray*, ch. 19; in "Phrases and Philosophies," Wilde writes: "No crime is vulgar, but all vulgarity is crime. Vulgarity is the conduct of others" (repr. in Ellmann, 434); the last sentence is spoken by Lord Goring in act 3 of *Husband*.

Crime belongs exclusively to the lower orders. I don't blame them in the smallest degree. I should fancy that crime was to them what art is to us, simply a method of procuring extraordinary sensations.

> Lord Henry in *Dorian Gray*, ch. 19.

Crime in England is rarely the result of sin. It is nearly always the result of starvation.

"Pen, Pencil, and Poison," in *Intentions* (1891), repr. in Ellmann, 337-38.

CRISIS

I have always been my own master; had at least always been so, till I met Dorian Gray. Then—but I don't know how to explain it to you. Something seemed to tell me that I was on the verge of a terrible crisis in my life. I had a strange feeling that Fate had in store for me exquisite joys and exquisite sorrows.

Basil Hallward in *Dorian Gray*, ch. 1.

CRITICS

The first condition of criticism is that the critic should be able to recognize that the sphere of Art and sphere of Ethics are absolutely distinct and separate. When they are confused, Chaos has come again. They are too often confused in England now, and though our modern Puritans cannot destroy a beautiful thing, yet, by means of their extraordinary prurience, they can almost taint beauty for a moment.

Gilbert in "The Critic as Artist," pt. 2, in *Intentions* (1891), repr. in Ellmann, 393.
The allusion to "Chaos" echoes *Othello*, act 3, sc. 3: "Chaos is come again."

The critic may, indeed, desire to exercise influence; but, if so, he will concern himself not with the individual, but with the age, which he will seek to wake into consciousness, and to make responsive, creating in it new desires and appetites, and lending it his larger vision and his nobler moods.

Gilbert in "The Critic as Artist," pt. 2, in *Intentions* (1891), repr. in Ellmann, 399-400.

CRITICISM

I would call criticism a creation within a creation. For just as the great artists, from Homer and Aeschylus, down to Shakespeare and Keats, did not go directly to life for their subject-matter, but sought for it in myth, and legend and ancient tale, so the critic deals with materials that others have, as it were, purified for him, and to which imaginative form and colour have been already added.

Gilbert in "The Critic as Artist," pt. 1, in *Intentions* (1891), repr. in Ellmann, 365.

A critic cannot be fair in the ordinary sense of the word. It is only about things that do not interest one that one can give a really unbiassed opinion, which is no doubt the reason why an unbiassed opinion is always absolutely valueless.

Gilbert in "The Critic as Artist," pt. 2, in *Intentions* (1891), repr. in Ellmann, 392.

Criticism is no more to be judged by any low standard of imitation or resemblance than is the work of poet or sculptor. The critic occupies the same relation to the work of art that he criticises as the artist does to the visible world of form and colour, or the unseen world of passion and of thought.

Gilbert in "The Critic as Artist," pt. 1, in *Intentions* (1891), repr. in Ellmann, 364.

It is Criticism, again, that, by concentration, makes culture possible. It takes the cumbersome mass of creative work, and distils it into a finer essence. Who that desires to retain any sense of form could struggle through the monstrous multitudinous books that the world has produced, books in which thought stammers or ignorance brawls? The thread that is to guide us across the wearisome labyrinth is in the hands of Criticism.

Gilbert in "The Critic as Artist," pt. 2, in *Intentions* (1891), repr. in Ellmann, 403-04.

That is what the highest criticism really is, the record of one's own soul. It is more fascinating than history, as it is concerned simply with oneself. . . . It is the only civilized form of autobiography, as it deals not with the events, but with the thoughts of one's life; not with life's physical accidents of deed or circumstance, but with the spiritual moods and imaginative passions of the mind.

Gilbert in "The Critic as Artist," pt. 1, in *Intentions* (1891), repr. in Ellmann, 365.

It is remarkable how little art there is in the work of dramatic critics in England. You find column after column of description, but the critics rarely know how to praise an artistic work. The fact is, it requires an artist to praise art; any one can pick it to pieces.

Quoted in: "The Censure and *Salomé*," *Pall Mall Budget* (June 20, 1892), repr. in Mikhail, 1:188.

An interview after hearing that *Salomé* had been refused a license for the stage.

The highest as the lowest form of criticism is a mode of autobiography.

Dorian Gray, Preface.

A critic should be taught to criticise a work of art without making any reference to the personality of the author. This, in fact, is the beginning of criticism.

Letters, 260.

Written to the Editor, *St. James's Gazette,* on June 27, 1890 in defense of *Dorian Gray.*

The critic has to educate the public; the artist has to educate the critic.

Letters, 269.

Written to the Editor, *Scots Observer,* on August 13, 1890 in defense of *Dorian Gray.*

Real critics? Ah! how perfectly charming they would be. I am always waiting for their arrival. An inaudible school would be nice.

Quoted in: Gilbert Burgess's "*An Ideal Husband* at the Haymarket Theatre: A Talk with Mr. Oscar Wilde," *Sketch* (January 9, 1895), repr. in Mikhail 1:240.

CROWDS

Whenever I have gone there, there have been either so many people that I have not been able to see the pictures, which was dreadful, or so many pictures that I have not been able to see the people, which was worse.

Lord Henry in *Dorian Gray*, ch. 1.

Exhibitions at the Royal Academy of Art were major social events of the season.

CULTURE

Self-culture is the true ideal of man. Goethe saw it, and the immediate debt that we owe to Goethe is greater than the debt we owe to any man since Greek days. The Greeks saw it, and have left us, as their legacy to modern thought, the conception of the contemplative life as well as the critical method by which alone can that life be truly realized. It was the one thing that made the Renaissance great, and gave us Humanism.

Gilbert in "The Critic as Artist," pt. 2, in *Intentions* (1891), repr. in Ellmann, 387.

The aim of culture is not rebellion but peace, the valley perilous where ignorant armies clash by night being no dwelling-place meet for her to whom the gods have assigned the fresh uplands and sunny heights and clear, untroubled air.

"English Renaissance," pub. in *Miscellanies*, 248; the passage is echoed in "L'Envoi," in Rennell Rodd's *Rose Leaf and Apple Leaf* (1882), repr. in *Miscellanies*, 39.

Wilde borrows "where ignorant armies clash by night" from Matthew Arnold's "Dover Beach" (1867).

Cure

Nothing can cure the soul but the senses, just as nothing can cure the senses but the soul.

Lord Henry in *Dorian Gray*, ch. 2.

Cynicism

JACK: For heaven's sake, don't try to be cynical. It's perfectly easy to be cynical.

ALGERNON: My dear fellow, it isn't easy to be anything nowadays. There's such a lot of beastly competition about.

Earnest, act 1.

Dancing

We caught the tread of dancing feet,
We loitered down the moonlit street,
And stopped beneath the Harlot's house.
****
Like strange mechanical grotesques,
Making fantastic arabesques,
The shadows raced across the blind.

"The Harlot's House," in the *Dramatic Review* (April 11, 1885), repr. in *Poems* (1997).

*D*ANDYISM

Dandyism is the assertion of the absolute modernity of Beauty.

"A Few Maxims," repr. in *Letters*, 870.

The aphorism reappears in *Dorian Gray*, ch. 11.

CECILY: Why did you pretend to be my guardian's brother?

ALGERNON: In order that I might have an opportunity of meeting you.

CECILY (*To Gwendolen*): That certainly seems a satisfactory explanation, does it not?

GWENDOLEN: Yes, dear, if you can believe him.

CECILY: I don't. But that does not affect the wonderful beauty of his answer.

GWENDOLEN: True. In matters of grave importance, style, not sincerity is the vital thing.

Earnest, act 3.

Gwendolen's final remark expresses the play's dandiacal theme.

MABEL CHILTERN: Why do you call Lord Goring good-for-nothing?

LORD CAVERSHAM: Because he leads such an idle life.

MABEL: How can you say such a thing? Why, he rides in the Row at ten o'clock in the morning, goes to the Opera three times a week, changes his clothes at least five times a day, and dines out every night of the season. You don't call that leading an idle life, do you?

Husband, act 1.

Mabel describes the life of a dandy; the Row alludes to the road in Hyde Park called "Rotten Row," a fashionable mecca for equestrians and carriages.

I don't think Prince Paul's nature is such a mystery. He would stab his best friend for the sake of writing an epigram on his tombstone.

Czarevitch in *Vera*, act 2.

Talk to every woman as if you loved her, and to every man as if he bored you, and at the end of your first season you will have the reputation of possessing the most perfect social tact.

Lord Illingworth to Gerald in *A Woman*, act 3.

People nowadays are so absolutely superficial that they don't understand the philosophy of the superficial. . . . Sentiment is all very well for the button-hole. But the essential thing for a necktie is style. A well-tied tie is the first serious step in life.

Lord Illingworth in *A Woman*, act 3.

The philosophy of dandyism, which devotes precise attention to style in dress and expression.

*D*ANTE

Alas! my Dante! thou hast known the pain
Of meaner lives,—the exile's galling chain,
How steep the stairs within kings' houses are,
And all the petty miseries which mar
Man's nobler nature with the sense of wrong.
Yet this dull world is grateful for thy song. . . .

Ravenna, lines 93-98 (Oxford, 1878), repr. in *Poems* (1997).

A political exile from Florence, Dante died in Ravenna.

The almond-face which Giotto drew so well,
The weary face of Dante; —to this day,
Here in his place of resting, far away
From Arno's yellow waters, rushing down
Through the wide bridges of that fairy town. . . .

Ravenna, lines 86-90 (Oxford, 1878), repr. in *Poems* (1997).

Dante's tomb is in Ravenna, the city to which he went into political exile from Florence, through which the Arno River runs.

*D*ARWIN, *CHARLES*

The nineteenth century is a turning point in history simply on account of the work of two men, Darwin and Renan, the one the critic of the Book of Nature, the other the critic of the books of God. Not to recognize this is to miss the meaning of one of the most important eras in the progress of the world.

Gilbert in "The Critic as Artist," pt. 2, in *Intentions* (1891), repr. in Ellmann, 407.

Wilde alludes to Charles Darwin's *Origin in Species* (1859) on evolution, and Ernest Renan's five-volume *History of the Origins of Christianity* (1888-90).

DEATH

Death and vulgarity are the only two facts in the nineteenth century that one cannot explain away.

Lord Henry in *Dorian Gray*, ch. 19.

I have no terror of Death. It is the coming of Death that terrifies me.

Dorian in *Dorian Gray*, ch. 18.

There are few of us who have not sometimes wakened before dawn, either after one of those dreamless nights that make us almost enamoured of death, or one of those nights of horror and misshapen joy, when through the chambers of the brain sweep phantoms more terrible than reality itself, and instinct with that vivid life that lurks in all grotesques, and that lends to Gothic art its enduring vitality. . . .

Dorian Gray, ch. 11.

CHASUBLE: Was the cause of death mentioned?
JACK: A severe chill, it seems.
MISS PRISM: As a man sows, so shall he reap.
CHASUBLE: Charity, dear Miss Prism, charity! None of us are perfect. I myself am peculiarly susceptible to draughts.

Earnest, act 2.
Jack Worthing has been pretending that his imaginary brother is dead.

CHASUBLE: Your brother Ernest dead?
JACK: Quite dead.
MISS PRISM: What a lesson for him! I trust he will profit by it.

Earnest, act 2.
Jack Worthing has been pretending that his imaginary brother is dead.

Death and Love seem to walk on either hand as I go through life: they are the only things I think of, their wings shadow me.

Letters, 358.
Written to Alfred Douglas in July 1894.

The present style of burying and sorrowing for the dead seems to me to make grief grotesque, and to turn mourning to a mockery. . . . If a man needs an elaborate tombstone in order to remain in the memory of his country, it is clear that his living at all was an act of absolute superfluity.

Letters, 168-69.

Written to the Rev. J. Page Hopps on January 14, 1885.

Somehow, I don't think I shall live to see the new century. If another century began, and I was still alive, it would really be more than the English could stand.

Quoted in: Robert Sherard, *The Life of Oscar Wilde* (New York, 1906), 422.

Said to a French journalist three months before Wilde's death.

Yet all is well; he has but passed
To Life's appointed bourne:
And alien tears will fill for him
Pity's long-broken urn,
For his mourners will be outcast men,
And outcasts always mourn.

Reading Gaol, lines 529-34, repr. in *Poems* (1997).

"He" is the executed trooper; the last four lines of the quotation are inscribed on Jacob Epstein's monument over Wilde's grave in Père Lachaise cemetery in Paris.

*D*EBT

£762 for eating! How grossly materialistic! There can be little good in any young man who eats so much, and so often.

Miss Prism in the Gribsby episode in act 2 of *Earnest* (cut from the stage production), pub. in the New York Public Library four-act version (New York, 1956).

Miss Prism remarking on Algernon Moncrieff's debt.

It is only by not paying one's bills that one can hope to live in the memory of the commercial classes.

"Phrases and Philosophies," repr. in Ellmann, 434.

*D*EBUTS

There will have to be an inquest, of course, and you must not be mixed up in it. Things like that make a man fashionable in Paris. But in London people are so prejudiced. Here, one should never make one's *début* with a scandal. One should reserve that to give an interest to one's old age.

Lord Henry to Dorian in *Dorian Gray*, ch. 8.

Following the suicide of Sibyl Vane.

*D*ECADENCE

It is my golden book; I never travel anywhere without it; but it is the very flower of decadence: the last trumpet should have sounded the moment it was written.

Quoted in: "Four Years: 1887-1891," pt. 8, in *The Autobiography of W. B. Yeats* (New York, 1965); for a slightly different version, see Yeats's *Memoirs*, ed. Denis Donoghue (New York, 1973), 22.

On Walter Pater's noted *Studies in the History of the Renaissance* (1873).

*D*ECAY

Underneath the fanciful form it ["the decay of lying"] hides some truths, or perhaps some half-truths, about art, which I think require to be put forward, and of which some are, I think, quite new. . . . I have blown my trumpet against the gate of dullness. . . .

Letters, 237.

Written to the actress Kate Terry Lewis in January 1889.

*D*EGRADATION

There is not a single degradation of the body which I must not try and make into a spiritualising of the soul.

Letters, 469.

Written to Alfred Douglas in early 1897 from Reading Prison, partly pub. as *De Profundis* (1905).

We are all in the gutter, but some of us are looking at the stars.

Lord Darlington in *Fan*, act 3.

DEMOCRACY

High hopes were once formed of democracy; but democracy means simply the bludgeoning of the people by the people for the people. It has been found out. I must say that it was high time, for all authority is quite degrading.

"The Soul of Man," repr. in Ellmann, 266.

The passage beginning with "bludgeoning of the people" echoes Lincoln's "Gettysburg Address" (1863): "government of the people, by the people, and for the people. . . ."

[Democracy] degrades those who exercise it, and degrades those over whom it is exercised. When it is violently, grossly, and cruelly used, it produces a good effect, by creating, or at any rate bringing out, the spirit of revolt and individualism that is to kill it. When it is used with a certain amount of kindness, and accompanied by prizes and rewards, it is dreadfully demoralizing.

"The Soul of Man," repr. in Ellmann, 266-67.

DESPAIR

We were as men who through a fen
Of filthy darkness grope:
We did not dare to breathe a prayer,
Or to give our anguish scope:
Something was dead in each of us,
And what was dead was Hope.

Reading Gaol, lines 355-60, repr. in *Poems* (1997).

DESPOTISM

There are three kinds of despots. There is the despot who tyrannizes over the body. There is the despot who tyrannizes over the soul. There is the despot who tyrannizes over soul and body alike. The first is called the Prince. The second is called the Pope. The third is called the People.

"The Soul of Man," repr. in Ellmann, 282.

DESTINY

My cradle was rocked by the Fates. Only in the mire can I know peace.

Letters, 629.

Written to his friend Carlos Blacker in August 1897 from France.

Man's destiny is to be haunted; however deserted of his fellows, he is never for a moment alone.

Quoted in: Housman, 42.

DICKENS, CHARLES

Remembering that of all forms of error prophecy is the most gratuitous, we will not take upon ourselves to decide the question of Dickens's immortality. If our descendants do not read him they will miss a great source of amusement, and if they do, we hope they will not model their style upon his.

"A New Book on Dickens," in *PMG* (March 31, 1887), repr. in Ellmann, 48.

A review of Frank T. Marzials's *Life of Charles Dickens*.

Still, the fact remains that a man who was affectionate and loving to his children, generous and warm-hearted to his friends, and whose books are the very bacchanalia of benevolence, pilloried his parents to make the groundlings laugh, and this fact every biographer of Dickens should face and, if possible, explain.

"A New Book on Dickens," in *PMG* (March 31, 1887), repr. in Ellmann, 47.

A review of Frank T. Marzials's *Life of Charles Dickens* .

DILETTANTES

To the world I seem, by intention on my part, a dilettante and dandy merely—it is not wise to show one's heart to the world—and as seriousness of manner is the disguise of the fool, folly in its exquisite modes of triviality and indifference and lack of care is the robe of the wise man. In so vulgar an age as this we all need masks.

Letters, 353.

Written to the artist Philip Houghton in February 1894 .

DISCIPLES

Every great man nowadays has his disciples, and it is usually Judas who writes the biography.

"The Butterfly's Boswell," in *CSR* (April 20, 1887), repr. in Ellmann, 65; the aphorism reappears—with the change from "usually" to "always"—in "The Critic as Artist," pt. 1, in *Intentions* (1891), repr. in Ellmann, 342.

Whistler's "Boswell" was Walter Dowdeswell, who had published a favorable biographical article in *Art Journal* (April 1887).

DISCONTENT

Discontent is the first step in the progress of a man or a nation.

Lord Illingworth in *A Woman*, act 2.

DISHONESTY

JACK: It pains me very much to have to speak frankly to you, Lady Bracknell, about your nephew, but the fact is that I do not approve at all of his moral character. I suspect him of being untruthful.

LADY BRACKNELL: Untruthful! My nephew Algernon? Impossible! He is an Oxonian.

Earnest, act 3.

An "Oxonian" is a graduate of Oxford University.

DISOBEDIENCE

Disobedience, in the eyes of any one who has read history, is man's original virtue. It is through disobedience that progress has been made, through disobedience and through rebellion.

"The Soul of Man," repr. in Ellmann, 258.

DIVERSITY

As for the infinite variety of Nature, that is a pure myth. It is not be found in Nature herself. It resides in the imagination, or fancy, or cultivated blindness of the man who looks at her.

Vivian in "The Decay of Lying," in *Intentions* (1891), repr. in Ellmann, 291.

DIVORCE

Divorces are made in heaven.

Algernon Moncrieff in *Earnest*, act 1.

DOUBLE LIFE

Leading a double life is the only proper preparation for marriage.

Quoted in: Small, 145.

DRAMATISTS

The true dramatist aims first at what is characteristic, and no more desires that all his personages should be beautifully attired than he desires that they should all have beautiful natures or speak beautiful English. The true dramatist, in fact, shows us life under the conditions of art, not art in the form of life.

"The Truth of Masks," in *Intentions* (1891), repr. in Ellmann, 428.

DREAMERS

Yes, I am a dreamer. For a dreamer is one who can only find his way by moonlight, and his punishment is that he sees the dawn before the rest of the world.

Gilbert in "The Critic as Artist," pt. 2, in *Intentions* (1891), repr. in Ellmann, 407.

DULLNESS

I am but too conscious of the fact that we are born in an age when only the dull are treated seriously, and I live in terror of not being misunderstood.

Gilbert in "The Critic as Artist," pt. 1, in *Intentions* (1891), repr. in Ellmann, 349.

Dullness is the coming of age of seriousness.

"Phrases and Philosophies," repr. in Ellmann, 433.

DUTY

People are afraid of themselves, nowadays. They have forgotten the highest of all duties, the duty that one owes to one's self. Of course they are charitable. They feed the hungry, and clothe the beggar. But their own souls starve, and are naked.

Lord Henry in *Dorian Gray*, ch. 2.

The first duty in life is to be as artificial as possible. What the second duty is no one has as yet discovered.

"Phrases and Philosophies," repr. in Ellmann, 433.

Wilde's view of dandyism.

DYING

I am dying, as I have lived, beyond my means.

Quoted in: Hesketh Pearson, *Oscar Wilde: His Life and Wit* (New York, 1946), ch. 18.

On December 14, 1900, Robert Ross wrote to More Adey that Wilde "said he was 'dying above his means,'" though Ross does not say what prompted the remark (*Letters*, 847); the earliest published version of Wilde's famous remark is apparently that in Robert Sherard's *Life of Oscar Wilde* (New York, 1906), 421, reporting Wilde's reaction to a "huge fee" for an operation ("I suppose that I shall have to die beyond my means"); in Harris, ch. 26 (as in Pearson), Wilde responds to the cost of champagne (. . . "when it was brought [he] declared that he was dying as he had lived, 'beyond his means'").

ℰARNEST *(THE PLAY)*

This scene that you feel is superfluous cost me terrible exhausting labour
and heart-rending nerve-racking strain. You may not believe me, but I
assure you on my honour that it must have taken fully five minutes to
write.

Quoted in: Hesketh Pearson, *Oscar Wilde: His Life and Wit* (New York, 1946), ch. 18.

The actor and theater manager George Alexander had insisted that a scene (involving Gribsby
the solicitor) be cut from *Earnest* in order to reduce Wilde's original four-act version to three
acts.

ℰCCENTRICITY

It is now months since I discarded my eccentricities of costume and had
my hair cut. All that belonged to the Oscar of the first period. We are now
concerned with the Oscar Wilde of the second period, who has nothing
whatever in common with the gentleman who wore long hair and carried a
sunflower down Piccadilly.

Quoted in: Robert Sherard's *The Real Oscar Wilde* (1915), repr. in Mikhail 1:118.

ℰCONOMICS

Cecily, you will read your political economy in my absence. The chapter on
the Fall of the Rupee you may omit. It is somewhat too sensational. Even
these metallic problems have their melodramatic side.

Miss Prism in *Earnest*, act 2.

ℰCSTASY

Our most fiery moments of ecstasy are merely shadows of what somewhere
else we have felt, or of what we long some day to feel.

Letters, 185.

Written to H. C. Marillier, an acquaintance, in early 1886.

*E*DUCATION

Oh! my dear Ernest, to sit next a man who has spent his life in trying to educate others! What a dreadful experience that is! How appalling is that ignorance which is the inevitable result of the fatal habit of imparting opinions! How limited in range the creature's mind proves to be!

Gilbert in "The Critic as Artist," pt. 2, in *Intentions* (1891), repr. in Ellmann, 387.

If you meet at dinner a man who has spent his life in educating himself—a rare type in our time, I admit, but still one occasionally to be met with— you rise from table richer, and conscious that a high ideal has for a moment touched and sanctified your days.

Gilbert in "The Critic as Artist," pt. 2, in *Intentions* (1891), repr. in Ellmann, 386-87.

We, in our educational system, have burdened the memory with a load of unconnected fact, and laboriously striven to impart our laboriously-acquired knowledge. We teach people how to remember, we never teach them how to grow.

Gilbert in "The Critic as Artist," pt. 2, in *Intentions* (1891), repr. in Ellmann, 403.

In the false education of our present system, minds too young to grapple with the subjects in the right sense are burdened with those bloody slaughters and barbarous brawls of the French and English wars and that calendar of infamy, European history. How much better would it be in these early years to teach children in the useful branches of art, to use their hands in the rational service of mankind.

"The Decorative Arts," in O'Brien, 163.

The whole theory of modern education is radically unsound. Fortunately in England, at any rate, education produces no effect whatsoever. If it did, it would prove a serious danger to the upper classes, and probably lead to acts of violence in Grosvenor Square.

Lady Bracknell in *Earnest*, act 1.

Education is an admirable thing. But it is well to remember from time to time that nothing that is worth knowing can be taught.

"A Few Maxims," repr. in *Letters*, 869.

You and I, dear Mrs. Arbuthnot, are behind the age. . . . Too much care was taken with our education, I am afraid. To have been well brought up is a great drawback nowadays. It shuts one out from so much.

Lady Hunstanton in *A Woman*, act 3.

*E*GOTISM

Even in actual life egotism is not without its attractions. When people talk to us about others they are usually dull. When they talk to us about themselves they are nearly always interesting, and if one could shut them up, when they become wearisome, as easily as one can shut up a book of which one has grown wearied, they would be perfect absolutely.

Gilbert in "The Critic as Artist," pt. 1, in *Intentions* (1891), repr. in Ellmann, 342.

Egotism itself, which is so necessary to a proper sense of human dignity, is entirely the result of indoor life. Out of doors one becomes abstract and impersonal. One's individuality absolutely leaves one.

Vivian in "The Decay of Lying," in *Intentions* (1891), repr. in Ellmann, 291.

*E*LECT, THE

They are the elect to whom beautiful things mean only Beauty.

Dorian Gray, Preface.

*E*MOTIONS

The advantage of the emotions is that they lead us astray, and the advantage of Science is that it is not emotional.

Lord Henry in *Dorian Gray*, ch. 3.

*E*NEMIES

Ernest Harrowden, one of those middle-aged mediocrities so common in London clubs who have no enemies, but are thoroughly disliked by their friends. . . .

Dorian Gray, ch. 15.

In the periodical *United Ireland* (September 26, 1891), W. B. Yeats remarked that Wilde had said of "a certain notorious and clever, but coldblooded Socialist" (obviously Bernard Shaw): . . . "he has no enemies, but is intensely disliked by all his friends"; in *The Autobiography of W. B. Yeats* (New York, 1965), the remark reappears on p. 89, repr. in Mikhail 1:146.

Be careful to choose your enemies well. Friends don't much matter. But the choice of enemies is very important.

Quoted in: Vincent O'Sullivan, *Aspects of Wilde* (New York, 1936), 82.

*E*NGAGEMENTS

CECILY: Do you suggest, Miss Fairfax, that I entrapped Ernest into an engagement? How dare you? This is no time for wearing the shallow mask of manners. When I see a spade I call it a spade.
GWENDOLEN: I am glad to say that I have never seen a spade. It is obvious that our social spheres have been widely different.

Earnest, act 2.

To speak frankly, I am not in favour of long engagements. They give people the opportunity of finding out each other's character before marriage, which I think is never advisable.

Lady Bracknell in *Earnest*, act 3.

*E*NGLAND

We have really everything in common with America nowadays, except, of course, language.

"The Canterville Ghost," pt. 1, in *CSR* (February 23 and March 2, 1887), repr. in *Lord Arthur*.

LORD HENRY: Would you have me take the verdict of Europe on [England]?
DUCHESS OF MONMOUTH: What do they say of us?
LORD HENRY: That Tartuffe has emigrated to England and opened a shop.

Dorian Gray, ch. 17.

Tartuffe is the religious hypocrite in Moliere's play Le Tartuffe (l664).

England will never be civilized till she has added Utopia to her dominians. There is more than one of her colonies that she might with advantage surrender for so fair a land.

Gilbert in "The Critic as Artist," pt. 2, in Intentions (1891), repr. in Ellmann, 386.

In England a man who can't talk morality twice a week to a large, popular, immoral audience is quite over as a serious politician. There would be nothing left for him as a profession except Botany or the Church.

Lord Goring in Husband, act 2.

One has merely to read the ordinary English newspapers and the ordinary English novels of our day to become conscious of the fact that it is only the obvious that occurs, and only the obvious that is written about. Both facts are much to be regretted.

Letters, 295-96. Written to the Editor, PMG on August 27, 1891.

In England, the arts that have escaped best are the arts in which the public take no interest. Poetry is an instance of what I mean. We have been able to have fine poetry in England because the public do not read it, and consequently do not influence it.

"The Soul of Man," repr. in Ellmann, 271.

Just as the worst slave-owners were those who were kind to their slaves, and so prevented the horror of the system being realised by those who suffered from it, and understood by those who contemplated it, so, in the present state of things in England, the people who do most harm are the people who try to do most good. . . .

"The Soul of Man," repr. in Ellmann, 256.

There is not a single real poet or prose-writer of this century, for instance, on whom the British public have not solemnly conferred diplomas of immorality, and these diplomas practically take the place, with us, of what in France is the formal recognition of an Academy of Letters, and fortunately make the establishment of such an institution quite unnecessary in England.

"The Soul of Man," repr. in Ellmann, 273.

This mighty empire hath but feet of clay:
Of all its ancient chivalry and might
Our little island is forsaken quite:
Some enemy hath stolen its crown of bay

****

It mars my calm: wherefore in dreams of Art
And loftiest culture I would stand apart,
Neither for God, nor for his enemies.

> "Theoretikos," in *Poems* (1881), repr. in *Poems* (1997).

> The title means "The Contemplative"; in the 1870s, Wilde wrote several poems lamenting England's moral decline because of the Israeli government's reluctance to challenge Turkish misrule in the Balkans .

Seeing this little isle on which we stand,
This England, this sea-lion of the sea,
By ignorant demagogues is held in fee,
Who love her not: Dear God! is this the land
Which bare a triple empire in her hand
When Cromwell spake the word Democracy!

> "To Milton," in *Poems* (1881), repr. in *Poems* (1997).

> Commenting on England's moral decline, principally because of a non-interventionist policy concerning Turkish atrocities in Bulgaria in 1877.

When liberty comes with hands dappled in blood it is hard to shake hands with her. We forget how much England is to blame. She is reaping the fruit of seven centuries of injustice.

> Quoted in: the *Philadelphia Press* (May 9, 1882) during Wilde's American lecture tour; repr. in Lewis and Smith, 344.

> Wilde's response to the murder by the Fenians of the Irish chief secretary Lord Frederick Cavendish and T. H. Burke, the Irish under-secretary on May 6, in Dublin.

*E*NGLISH, THE

English people are far more interested in American barbarism than they are in American civilization.

> "The American Invasion," in *CSR* (March 23, 1887), repr. in Ellmann, 54.

[Our countrymen] are more cunning than practical. When they make up their ledger, they balance stupidity by wealth, and vice by hypocrisy.

> Lord Henry in *Dorian Gray*, ch. 17.

To disagree with three-fourths of the British public on all points is one of the first elements of sanity, one of the deepest consolations in all moments of spiritual doubt.

"English Renaissance," pub. in *Miscellanies*, 250.

The English are always degrading truths into facts. When a truth becomes a fact it loses all its intellectual value.

"A Few Maxims," repr. in *Letters*, 869.

If one could only teach the English how to talk, and the Irish how to listen, society here would be quite civilized.

Mrs. Cheveley in *Husband*, act 3.

With all your pomp and wealth and art you don't know how to live—you don't even know that. You love the beauty that you can see and touch and handle, the beauty that you can destroy, and do destroy, but of the unseen beauty of life, of the unseen beauty of a higher life, you know nothing. You have lost life's secret. Oh, your English society seems to me shallow, selfish, foolish.

Hester Worsley in *A Woman*, act 2.

I do not deny that Englishmen possess certain practical qualities; but, as I am an artist, these qualities are not those which I can admire. Moreover, I am not at present an Englishman. I am an Irishman, which is by no means the same thing.

Quoted in: Maurice Sisley's "La *Salomé* de M. Oscar Wilde," *Le Gaulois* (June 29, 1892), repr. in Mikhail, 1:190.
Remarks made when *Salomé* had been refused a license for the stage.

When at the end of each year the English make up their national ledger, they balance their stupidity by their wealth, and their vices by their hypocrisy.

Quoted in: Small, 128.

The English are the most extraordinarily hardworking race. They are the only nation now left in Europe that takes the trouble to be hypocritical.

Quoted in: Small, 128.

ENVIRONMENT

We try to improve the conditions of the race by means of good air, free sunlight, wholesome water, and hideous bare buildings for the better housing of the lower orders. But these things merely produce health, they do not produce beauty. For this, Art is required, and the true disciples of the great artist are not his studio-imitators, but those who become like his works of art . . . in a word, Life is Art's best, Art's only pupil.

Vivian in "The Decay of Lying," in *Intentions* (1891), repr. in Ellmann, 308.

If you go into a house where everything is coarse and you find the common cups chipped and the saucers cracked, it will often be because the children have an utter contempt for them, but if everything is dainty and delicate, you teach them practically what beauty is, and gentleness and refinement of manner are unconsciously acquired.

"The Decorative Arts," in O'Brien, 162.

EQUALITY

GWENDOLYN: How absurd to talk of the equality of the sexes! Where
    questions of self-sacrifice are concerned, men are infinitely beyond us.
JACK: We are!
CECILY: They have moments of physical courage of which we women know
    absolutely nothing.

Earnest, act 3.

Responses to Jack Worthing and Algernon Moncrieff's determination to endure baptism in order to change their names to "Ernest."

ERRORS

The fatal errors of life are not due to man's being unreasonable: an unreasonable moment may be one's finest moment. They are due to man's being logical. There is a wide difference.

Letters, 446.

Written to Alfred Douglas in early 1897 from Reading Prison, partly pub. as *De Profundis* (1905).

$\mathcal{E}VIL$

CARDINAL: There seem many evils in this town, which in your wisdom
    might your Grace reform.
FIRST CITIZEN: What is that word reform? What does it mean?
SECOND CITIZEN: Marry, it means leaving things as they are. . . .

Duchess, act 2.

People thought it dreadful of me to have entertained at dinner the evil
things of life, and to have found pleasure in their company. But they, from
the point of view through which I, as an artist in life, approached them,
were delightfully suggestive and stimulating. It was like feasting with
panthers. The danger was half the excitement.

Letters, 492.

Written to Alfred Douglas in early 1897 from Reading Prison, partly pub. as *De Profundis*
(1905).

$\mathcal{E}VOLUTION$

"The Chronicle of Mites" is a mock-heroic poem about the inhabitants of a
decaying cheese, who speculate about the origin of their species, and hold
learned discussions upon the meaning of Evolution, and the Gospel
according to Darwin. This cheese-epic is a rather unsavoury production,
and the style is, at times, so monstrous and so realistic that the author
should be called the Gorgon-Zola of literature.

"The Poets' Corner," in *PMG* (February 15, 1888), repr. in Ellmann, 85.

The author of the "cheese-epic" is James Aitchison; Wilde's pun at the end combines the
monstrous Gorgon (of Greek myth) and Zola (the "realistic" novelist).

$\mathcal{E}XAMINATIONS$

In examinations the foolish ask questions that the wise cannot answer.

"Phrases and Philosophies," repr. in Ellmann, 434.

EXECUTION

At six o'clock we cleaned our cells,
At seven all was still,
But the sough and swing of a mighty wing
The prison seemed to fill,
For the Lord of Death with icy breath
Had entered in to kill.

> *Reading Gaol*, lines 343-48, repr. in *Poems* (1997)
>
> Hangings were customarily carried out at 8 AM; the Lord of Death is the Angel of Death with its "mighty wing."

EXERCISE

If it were not for the running-ground at Eton, the towing-path at Oxford, the Thames swimming baths, and the yearly circuses, humanity would forget the plastic perfection of its own form, and degenerate into a race of short-sighted professors and spectacled *précieuses*!

> "London Models," *English Illustrated Magazine* (January 1889), repr. in Ellmann, 114.

EXPERIENCE

Experience was of no ethical value. It was merely the name men gave to their mistakes.

> Prince Paul in *Vera*, act 2, the epigram echoed by Dumby in *Fan*, act 3.

EXPERIMENT

It often happened that when we thought we were experimenting on others we were really experimenting on ourselves.

> *Dorian Gray*, ch. 4.

FACTS

If something cannot be done to check, or at least to modify, our monstrous worship of facts, Art will become sterile, and Beauty will pass away from the land.

> Vivian in "The Decay of Lying," in *Intentions* (1891), repr. in Ellmann, 294-95.

Facts are not merely finding a footing-place in history, but they are usurping the domain of Fancy, and have invaded the kingdom of Romance. Their chilling touch is over everything. They are vulgarising mankind.

> Vivian in "The Decay of Lying," in *Intentions* (1891), repr. in Ellmann, 304.

FAILURES

How fascinating all failures are!

> *Letters*, 122.
> Written to the author Julia Ward Howe on July 6, 1882 in reference to the American soldier and statesman Jefferson Davis..

FAITHFULNESS

Faithfulness is to the emotional life what consistency is to the life of the intellect—simply a confession of failure.

> Lord Henry in *Dorian Gray*, ch. 4.

Those who are faithful know only the trivial side of love: it is the faithless who know love's tragedies.

> Lord Henry in *Dorian Gray*, ch. 1.

FAME

Somehow or other I'll be famous, and, if not famous, I'll be notorious.

> Quoted in: David Hunter-Blair, *In Victorian Days and Other Papers* (New York, 1939), repr. in Mikhail 1:5.
> Blair was a friend of Wilde at Oxford University.

FAMILY

Mr. Worthing, I confess I feel somewhat bewildered by what you have just told me. To be born, or at any rate bred, in a hand-bag, whether it had handles or not, seems to me to display a contempt for the ordinary decencies of family life that reminds one of the worst excesses of the French Revolution. And I presume you know what that unfortunate movement led to?

Lady Bracknell in *Earnest*, act 1.

FATE

There is a fatality about all physical and intellectual distinction, the sort of fatality that seems to dog through history the faltering steps of kings. It is better not to be different from one's fellows.

Basil Hallward in *Dorian Gray*, ch. 1.

FAULTS

How charming you are, dear Lord Illingworth. You always find out that one's most glaring fault is one's most important virtue.

Lady Hunstanton in *A Woman*, act 3.

FICTION

Anybody can write a three-volumed novel. It merely requires a complete ignorance of both life and literature.

Gilbert in "The Critic as Artist," pt. 1, in *Intentions* (1891), repr. in Ellmann, 358.

As for that great and daily increasing school of novelists for whom the sun always rises in the East-End, the only thing that can be said about them is that they find life crude, and leave it raw.

Vivian in "The Decay of Lying," in *Intentions* (1891), repr. in Ellmann, 296.

Wilde alludes to the realistic novelists emphasizing sordidness.

His eye fell on the yellow book that Lord Henry had sent him. . . . It was a novel without a plot, and with only one character, being, indeed, simply a psychological study of a certain young Parisian, who spent his life trying to realize in the nineteenth century all the passions and modes of thought that belonged to every century except his own, and to sum up, as it were, in himself the various moods through which the world-spirit had ever passed. . . .

> *Dorian Gray*, ch. 10.
>
> In a letter (see *Letters*, 313), Wilde said that the "yellow book" was "partly suggested" by Joris-Karl Huysmans's *A Rebours* (1884).

There were in it metaphors as monstrous as orchids, and as subtle in colour. The life of the senses was described in the terms of mystical philosophy. One hardly knew at times whether one was reading the spiritual ecstasies of some mediaeval saint or the morbid confessions of a modern sinner. It was a poisonous book.

> *Dorian Gray*, ch. 10.
>
> A description of the "yellow book," which Lord Henry had given to Dorian, partly suggested, as Wilde said (see *Letters*, 313), by Joris-Karl Huysmans's *A Rebours* (1884).

MISS PRISM: Do not speak slightingly of the three-volume novel, Cecily. I wrote one myself in earlier days.

CECILY: Did you really, Miss Prism? . . . I hope it did not end happily? I don't like novels that end happily. They depress me so much.

MISS PRISM: The good ended happily, and the bad unhappily. That is what Fiction means.

> *Earnest*, act 2.

It is quite tragic for me to think how completely *Dorian Gray* has been understood on all sides!

> *Letters*, 343.
>
> Written to the parodist and novelist Ada Leverson in July 1893.

*F*IN DE SIÈCLE

All that is known by that term [*fin de siècle*] I particularly admire and love. It is the fine flower of our civilisation: the only thing that keeps the world from the commonplace, the coarse, the barbarous.

> *More Letters*, 123.
>
> Written to the Tory journalist Leo Maxse in 1894; the term *fin de siècle* was associated with artistic Decadence.

FLAUBERT, GUSTAVE

Flaubert did not write French prose, but the prose of a great artist who happened to be French.

Letters, 233.

Written to the poet W. E. Henley in December 1888.

FLOWERS: GREEN

Thou wilt do this thing for me, Narraboth, and tomorrow when I pass in my litter beneath the gateway of the idol-sellers I will let fall for thee a little flower, a little green flower.

Salome in *Salome* (1894).

Urging Narraboth to bring Iokanaan out of the cistern so that she may see him; the green flower suggesting the Decadent green carnation that Wilde sometimes wore.

FOG

Now it must be admitted, fogs are carried to excess. They have become the mere mannerism of a clique, and the exaggerated realism of their method gives dull people bronchitis. Where the cultured catch an effect, the uncultured catch cold. And so, let us be humane, and invite Art to turn her wonderful eyes elsewhere.

Vivian in "The Decay of Lying," in *Intentions* (1891), repr. in Ellmann, 312.

The "clique" refers to the Impressionists.

FOLK-TALE

The Folk-tale is the father of all fiction, as the Folk-song is the mother of all poetry; and in the games, the tales and the ballads of primitive people it is easy to see the germs of such perfected forms of art as the drama, the novel and the epic.

"The Poetry of the People," in *PMG* (May 13, 1886), repr. in *Reviews*, 63.

FOREIGNERS

You have never been to any of my parties, have you, Mr. Gray? You must
come. I can't afford orchids, but I spare no expense in foreigners. They
make one's rooms look so picturesque.

Lord Henry's wife in *Dorian Gray*, ch. 4.

FORGIVENESS

Out of his mouth a red, red rose!
Out of his heart a white!
For who can say by what strange way,
Christ brings His will to light,
Since the barren staff the pilgrim bore
Bloomed in the great Pope's sight?

Reading Gaol, lines 481-86, repr. in *Poems* (1997).

The blooming of symbolic flowers from the trooper's corpse is here associated with the
legendary Tannhäuser, to whom the Pope said that forgiveness for the troubadour's sinful
dalliance with Venus was as impossible as roses blooming on the pilgrim's staff, but when it
bloomed, Tannhäuser could not be found.

FORM

From time to time the world cries out against some charming artistic poet,
because, to use its hackneyed and silly phrase, he has "nothing to say." But
if he had something to say, he would probably say it, and the result would
be tedious. It is just because he has no new message, that he can do
beautiful work. He gains his inspiration from form, and from form purely,
as an artist should. A real passion would ruin him.

Gilbert in "The Critic as Artist," pt. 2, in *Intentions* (1891), repr. in Ellmann, 398.

It is not merely in art that the body is the soul. In every sphere of life Form
is the beginning things. . . . Yes: Form is everything. It is the secret of life.
Find expression for a sorrow, and it will become dear to you. Find

expression for a joy, and you intensify its ecstasy . . . to return to the sphere of Art, it is Form that creates not merely the critical temperament, but also the aesthetic instinct, that unerring instinct that reveals to one all things under their conditions of beauty.

Gilbert in "The Critic as Artist," pt. 2, in *Intentions* (1891), repr. in Ellmann, 399.

Yes, the objective form is the most subjective in matter. Man is least himself when he talks in his own person. Give him a mask, and he will tell you the truth.

Gilbert in "The Critic as Artist," pt. 2, in *Intentions* (1891), repr. in Ellmann, 389.

*F*RANCE

In France, in fact, they limit the journalist, and allow the artist almost perfect freedom. *Here we allow absolute freedom to the journalist, and entirely limit the artist.*

"The Soul of Man," repr. in Ellmann, 277.

I was thinking in bed this morning that the great superiority of France over England is that in France every bourgeois wants to be an artist, whereas in England every artist wants to be a bourgeois.

Quoted in: Vincent O'Sullivan, *Aspects of Wilde* (New York, 1936), 64.

*F*REEDOM

To be entirely free, and at the same time entirely dominated by law, is the eternal paradox of human life that we realise at every moment. . . .

Letters, 443.

Written to Alfred Douglas in early 1897 from Reading Prison, partly pub. as *De Profundis* (1905).

FRIENDS

I choose my friends for their good looks, my acquaintances for their good characters, and my enemies for their good intellects. A man cannot be too careful in the choice of his enemies.

Lord Henry in *Dorian Gray*, ch. 1.

Friends who are also poets are never forgotten: memory keeps them in rose-leaves: but Life—coloured, turbulent Life—rushes like a river between oneself and those whom one likes, too often.

Letters, 378.
Written to the poet G. H. Kersley on November 21, 1894.

I would sooner lose my best friend than my worst enemy. To have friends, you know, one need only be good-natured; but when a man has no enemy left there must be something mean about him.

Prince Paul in *Vera*, act 2.

Know him? I know him so well that I haven't spoken to him in ten years.

Quoted in: Vincent O'Sullivan, *Aspects of Wilde* (New York, 1936), 87.
On being asked whether he knew the novelist George Moore.

FRIENDSHIP

Friendship is far more tragic than love. It lasts longer.

"A Few Maxims," repr. in *Letters*, 869.

To me the mirror of perfect friendship can never be dulled by any treachery, however mean, or disloyalty, however base. Individuals come and go like shadows but the ideal remains untarnished always. . . .

Letters, 146-47.
Written to Wilde's earliest biographer Robert Sherard in May 1883.

GENEROSITY

People are very fond of giving away what they need most themselves. It is
what I call the depth of generosity.

Lord Henry in *Dorian Gray*, ch. 4.

Dorian had remarked that Basil Hallward gives him good advice.

We think that we are generous because we credit our neighbour with the
possession of those virtues that are likely to be a benefit to us. We praise
the banker that we may overdraw our account, and find good qualities in
the highwayman in the hope that he may spare our pockets.

Lord Henry in *Dorian Gray*, ch. 6.

GENIUS

I have put my genius into my life; I have put only my talent into my works.

André Gide quoting Wilde in a letter dated January 30, 1895 in *Correspondance avec sa mère, 1880-1895*,
ed. C. Martin (1988), 590; the remark reappears in Gide's "Oscar Wilde: In Memoriam," *L'Ermitage*
(June 1902).

I have nothing to declare except my genius.

Quoted in: Harris, ch. 5.

Responding to a customs official upon arriving in New York in 1882.

GENIUSES

Geniuses talk so much, don't they? Such a bad habit! And they are always
thinking about themselves, when I want them to be thinking about me.

Mabel Chiltern in *Husband*, act 2.

GIDE, ANDRÉ

Listen, my dear friend, you must promise me one thing. Your *Nourritures Terrestres* is good, very good, but promise me you will never write a capital "I" again. In Art, you see, there is no first person.

Quoted in: Gide, ch. 3.
Gide's 1897 novel is translated *Fruits of the Earth.*

GOD

God and other artists are always a little obscure.

Letters, 379.
Written to the parodist and novelist Ada Leverson in December 1894.

No man can tell how God worketh. His ways are very dark. It may be that things which we call evil are good, and that the things which we call good are evil. There is no knowledge of anything. We can but bow our heads to His will, for God is very strong.

The fifth Jew in *Salomé* (1894).

GODS, THE

The gods are strange. It is not of our vices only they make instruments to scourge us. They bring us to ruin through what in us is good, gentle, humane, loving.

Letters, 440.
Written to Alfred Douglas in early 1897 from Reading Prison, partly pub. as *De Profundis* (1905); the second sentence echoes *King Lear*, act 5, sc. 3.

GOETHE, JOHANN VON

Among the many debts which we owe to the supreme aesthetic faculty of Goethe is that he was the first to teach us to define beauty in terms the most concrete possible, to realise it, I mean, always in its special manifestations.

"English Renaissance," pub. in *Miscellanies*, 243.

Goodness

Anybody can be good in the country. There are no temptations there. That is the reason why people who live out of town are so absolutely uncivilized.

Lord Henry in *Dorian Gray*, ch. 19.

To be good is to be in harmony with one's self. . . . Discord is to be forced to be in harmony with others.

Lord Henry in *Dorian Gray*, ch. 6.

Do you know I am afraid that good people do a great deal of harm in this world. Certainly the greatest harm they do is that they make badness of such extraordinary importance.

Lord Darlington in *Fan*, act 1.

Gossip

There is only one thing in the world worse than being talked about, and that is not being talked about.

Lord Henry in *Dorian Gray*, ch. 1.

Government

People sometimes inquire what form of government is most suitable for an artist to live under. To this question there is only one answer. *The form of government that is most suitable to the artist is no government at all.*

"The Soul of Man," repr. in Ellmann, 282.

Wilde's view of anarchism (the elimination of "government").

GRAVES

In Reading gaol by Reading town
There is a pit of shame,
And in it lies a wretched man
Eaten by teeth of flame,
In a burning winding-sheet he lies,
And his grave has got no name.

> *Reading Gaol*, lines 637-42, repr. in *Poems* (1997).
>
> The hanged trooper was buried in a pit of lime in the prison yard.

GREEK DRAMATISTS

Two crownèd Kings, and One that stood alone
With no green weight of laurels round his head,
But with sad eyes as one uncomforted,
And wearied with man's never-ceasing moan
For sins no bleating victim can atone,
And sweet long lips of tears and kisses fed.

> "A Vision," in the Dublin *Kottabos* (Hilary term 1877), repr. in *Poems* (1997).
>
> The "Kings" are the dramatists Aeschylus and Sophocles, triumphant at the annual Dionysian competitions; Euripides, who "stood alone," did not win many laurel wreaths, perhaps because of his criticism of Greek institutions.

GREEK TRAGEDY

I must admit that this thing that has happened does not affect me as it should. It seems to me to be simply like a wonderful ending to a wonderful play. It has all the terrible beauty of a Greek tragedy, a tragedy in which I took a great part, but by which I have not been wounded.

> Dorian to Lord Henry in *Dorian Gray*, ch. 8.
>
> On Sibyl Vane's suicide.

*G*REEK ART

It is strange, Greek art was the expression of joy. Modern art is a flower of suffering. Even Keats, who was almost Greek and gave his heart to the Nightingale, even Keats died of sorrow.

Quoted in: Charles Ricketts, *Oscar Wilde: Recollections* (1932), ch. 2.

*G*RIEF

[Madame de Ferrol] is really wonderful, and full of surprises. Her capacity for family affection is extraordinary. When her third husband died, her hair turned quite gold from grief.

Dorian Gray, ch. 15.

In *Earnest*, act 1, Algernon Moncrieff reports another grieving widow whose hair similarly turned to gold.

*H*AGGARD, RIDER

As for Mr. Rider Haggard, who really has, or had once, the makings of a perfectly magnificent liar, he is now so afraid of being suspected of genius that when he does tell us anything marvellous, he feels bound to invent a personal reminiscence, and to put it into a footnote as a kind of cowardly corroboration.

Vivian in "The Decay of Lying," in *Intentions* (1891), repr. in Ellmann, 295.

*H*ANDICRAFTS

Good handicrafts are due to guilds, not to the people. The moment the guilds lost their power and the people rushed in, beauty and honesty of work died.

"Lecture to Art Students," of the Royal Academy (June 30, 1883), pub. in *Miscellanies*, 315.

HAPPINESS

I have never searched for happiness. Who wants happiness? I have searched for pleasure.

Dorian in *Dorian Gray*, ch. 17.

The happiness of a married man depends on the people he has not married.

Lord Illingworth in *A Woman*, act 3.

HEALTH

One knows so well the popular idea of health. The English country gentleman galloping after a fox—the unspeakable in full pursuit of the uneatable.

Lord Illingworth in *A Woman*, act 1.

HEAVEN

GOD: Wherefore can I not send thee unto Heaven, and for what reason?
MAN: Because never, and in no place, have I been able to imagine it.

"The House of Judgment," lines 58-61, in the *Spirit Lamp* (February 17, 1893), repr. in *Poems* (1997).

HEDONISM

CYRIL: Whom do you mean by "the elect"?
VIVIAN: Oh, The Tired Hedonists of course. It is a club to which I belong. We are supposed to wear faded roses in our button-holes when we meet, and to have a sort of cult for Domitian. I am afraid you are not eligible. You are too fond of simple pleasures.

"The Decay of Lying," in *Intentions* (1891), repr. in Ellmann, 293.

Domitian, who, in AD 81, became a Roman emperor, was noted for his cruelty.

Yes: there was to be, as Lord Henry had prophesied, a new Hedonism that was to recreate life and to save it from that harsh uncomely puritanism that is having, in our own day, its curious revival. It was to have its service of the intellect, certainly, yet it was never to accept any theory or system that would involve the sacrifice of any mode of passionate experience. Its aim, indeed, was to be experience itself, and not the fruits of experience, sweet or bitter as they might be.

Dorian Gray, ch. 11.

Walter Pater's "Conclusion" to *Studies in the History of the Renaissance* (1873) is echoed in the final sentence.

*H*ELLENISM

It is really from the union of Hellenism, in its breadth, its sanity of purpose, its calm possession of beauty, with the adventive, the intensified individualism, the passionate colour of the romantic spirit, that spring the art of the nineteenth century in England. . . .

"English Renaissance," pub. in *Miscellanies*, 244.

*H*EROES

Formerly we used to canonize our heroes. The modern method is to vulgarize them. Cheap editions of great books may be delightful, but cheap editions of great men are absolutely detestable.

Gilbert in "The Critic as Artist," pt. 1, in *Intentions* (1891), repr. in Ellmann, 342.

Not a deed of heroism done on either continent in this century is fitly portrayed on canvas, and yet the history of a country should live on canvas and in marble as well as in dreary volumes; the history of Italy, of Holland, and, for a time, that of our own England, was told in speaking marble and living paintings.

"The Decorative Arts," in O'Brien, 156.

ℋEROISM

How few understand what a life of heroism is that of an artist when he is producing—not his art, but the receptacle which is to contain it. That, dear friends, is why the world is to the artist so tragic. It is always a struggle.

Quoted in: Housman, 38.

ℋISTORY

History is the account of the mutual attraction and repulsion of primitive political atoms. The atomic theory is a valuable hypothesis not merely in physics but in politics as well.

"Commonplace Book," pub. in Smith and Helfand, 117.

The one duty we owe to history is to rewrite it. That is not the least of the tasks in store for the critical spirit.

Gilbert in "The Critic as Artist," pt. 1, in *Intentions* (1891), repr. in Ellmann, 359.

We discover, remember, often enough, how constantly the history of a great nation will live in and by its art; only a few thin wreaths of beaten gold are all that remain to tell us of the stately empire of Etruria; and while from the streets of Florence the noble knight and haughty duke have long since passed away, the gates which the simple goldsmith, Ghiberti, made for their pleasure still guard their lovely house of baptism. . . .

"The Decorative Arts," in O'Brien, 161.

As he looked back upon man moving through History, he was haunted by a feeling of loss. So much had been surrendered! and to such little purpose! There had been mad wilful rejections, monstrous forms of self-torture and self-denial, whose origin was fear, and whose result was a degradation infinitely more terrible than that fancied degradation from which, in their ignorance, they had sought to escape. . . .

Dorian Gray, ch. 11.

On Dorian's obsession with self-denial.

History, no doubt, has splendid lessons for our instruction, just as all good art comes to us as the herald of the noblest truth. But, to set before either the painter or the historian the inculcation of moral lessons as an aim to be consciously pursued, is to miss entirely the true motive and characteristic of art and history, which is in the one case the creation of beauty, in the other the discovery of the laws of the evolution of progress. . . .

"Historical Criticism," pt. 2.

History ends with a few bare facts; Religion with a few undeniable Doctrines—beyond that all is invention.

Quoted in: Percival Almy's "New Views of Mr. Oscar Wilde," *Theatre* (March 1894), repr. in Mikhail 1:231.

$\mathcal{H}$OLY FAMILY, THE

Fawn at my feet fantastic Sphinx! and sing me all your memories! Sing to
    me of the Jewish maid who wandered with the Holy Child,
And how you led them through the wild, and how they slept beneath your
    shade.

The Sphinx, lines 31-32 (1894), repr. in *Poems* (1997).

$\mathcal{H}$OMOSEXUALITY

To have altered my life would have been to have admitted that Uranian [i.e., homosexual] love is ignoble. I hold it to be noble—more noble than other forms.

Letters, 705.

Written to Robert Ross in February 1898 from France.

$\mathcal{H}$ONOR

Ernest has a strong upright nature. He is the very soul of truth and honour. Disloyalty would be as impossible to him as deception. But even men of the noblest possible moral character are extremely susceptible to the influence of the physical charms of others. Modern, no less than Ancient History, supplies us with many most painful examples of what I refer to. If it were not so, indeed, History would be quite unreadable.

Gwendolen Fairfax in *Earnest*, act 2.

In the play's complex plot, Gwendolen, like Cecily, is unaware that Jack Worthing is also Ernest, whom Gwendolen has just discovered is Cecily's guardian.

$\mathcal{H}$OSTESSES

My dear fellow, she tried to found a *salon*, and only succeeded in opening a restaurant.

Lord Henry in *Dorian Gray*, ch. 1.

Commenting on the society hostess Lady Brandon.

$\mathcal{H}$OUSES AND HOMES

The home seems to me to be the proper sphere for the man. And certainly once a man begins to neglect his domestic duties he becomes painfully effeminate, does he not? And I don't like that. It makes men so very attractive.

Gwendolen Fairfax in *Earnest*, act 2.

$\mathcal{H}$UGHES, WILLIE

In Willie Hughes, Shakespeare found not merely a most delicate instrument for the presentation of his art, but the visible incarnation of his idea of beauty, and it is not too much to say that to this young actor, whose very name the dull writers of his age forgot to chronicle, the Romantic Movement of English Literature is largely indebted.

Mr. W. H., pt. 2, repr. in Ellmann, 187.

$\mathcal{H}$UMANISM

[Humanism] is the one thing that could make our own age great also; for the real weakness of England lies, not in incomplete armaments or unfortified coasts, not in the poverty that creeps through sunless lanes, or the drunkenness that brawls in loathsome courts, but simply in the fact that her ideals are emotional and not intellectual.

Gilbert in "The Critic as Artist," pt. 2, in *Intentions* (1891), repr. in Ellmann, 387.

$\mathcal{H}$UMANITY

It is because Humanity has never known where it was going that it has been able to find its way.

Gilbert in "The Critic as Artist," pt. 1, in *Intentions* (1891), repr. in Ellmann, 359.

Humanity takes itself too seriously. It is the world's original sin. If the caveman had known how to laugh, History would have been different.

Lord Henry in *Dorian Gray*, ch. 3.

$\mathcal{H}$UMILITY

Humility in the artist is his frank acceptance of all experiences, just as Love in the artist is simply that sense of Beauty that reveals to the world its body and its soul.

Letters, 476.

Written to Alfred Douglas in early 1897 from Reading Prison, partly pub. as *De Profundis* (1905).

$\mathcal{H}$USBANDS

It's most dangerous nowadays for a husband to pay any attention to his wife in public. It always makes people think that he beats her when they're alone. The world has grown so suspicious of anything that looks like a happy married life.

Lady Plymdale in *Fan*, act 2.

An ideal husband! Oh, I don't think I should like that. It sounds like something in the next world.

Mabel Chiltern in *Husband*, act 4.

*H*UYSMANS, JORIS-KARL

I have never read any of Huysmans' works, but he must be a great artist, because he has selected a monastery as his retreat. It is delightful see God through stained-glass windows.

Quoted in: Chris Healy's *Confessions of a Journalist* (1904), repr. in Mikhail, 2:385.

After his release from prison in May 1897, Wilde made the acquaintance of Healy and had, by that time, already read Huysmans's *A Rebours* (1884) and *En Route* (1895), which depicts a religious retreat from the world: see *Letters*, 313 and 520-21.

*I*DEAL MAN

After a whole dreadful week, during which one has gone about everywhere with one's husband, just to show how absolutely lonely one was, [the Ideal Man] may be given a third last parting, in the evening, and then, if his conduct has been quite irreproachable, and one has behaved really badly to him, he should be allowed to admit that he has been entirely in the wrong, and when he has admitted that, it becomes a woman's duty to forgive, and one can do it all over again from the beginning, with variations.

Mrs. Allonby in *A Woman*, act 2.

[The Ideal Man] should persistently compromise us in public, and treat us with absolute respect when we are alone. And yet he should be always ready to have a perfectly terrible scene, whenever we want one, and to become miserable, absolutely miserable, at a moment's notice, and to overwhelm us with just reproaches in less than twenty minutes, and to be positively violent at the end of half an hour. . . .

Mrs. Allonby in *A Woman*, act 2.

If we ask [the Ideal Man] a question about anything, he should give us an answer all about ourselves. He should invariably praise us for whatever qualities he knows we haven't got. But he should be pitiless, quite pitiless, in reproaching us for the virtues that we have never dreamed of possessing.

Mrs. Allonby in *A Woman*, act 2.

*I*DEALISM: GREEK

I believe that if one man were to live out his life fully and completely, were to give form to every feeling, expression to every thought, reality to every dream—I believe that the world would gain such a fresh impulse of joy that we would forget all the maladies of mediaevalism, and return to the Hellenic ideal—to something finer, richer, than the Hellenic ideal, it may be.

Lord Henry in *Dorian Gray*, ch. 2.

*I*DEALISM

We live, as I hope you know, Mr. Worthing, in an age of ideals. The fact is constantly mentioned in the more expensive monthly magazines, and has reached the provincial pulpits I am told: and my ideal has always been to love some one of the name of Ernest. There is something in that name that inspires absolute confidence.

Gwendolen Fairfax in *Earnest*, act 1.

The pun on "Ernest" would suggest to Victorian audiences the ideal of moral earnestness.

*I*DEAS

He played with the idea, and grew wilful; tossed it into the air and transformed it; let it escape and recaptured it; made it iridescent with fancy, and winged it with paradox.

Dorian Gray, ch. 3.

A description of Lord Henry's verbal facility.

𝓘DENTITIES

[*Dorian Gray*] contains much of me in it. Basil Hallward is what I think I am: Lord Henry what the world thinks me: Dorian what I would like to be—in other ages, perhaps.

Letters, 352.
Written to Ralph Payne (unidentified) in February 1894.

𝓘DLENESS

I am afraid I can't take him with me to Downing Street. It is not the Prime Minister's day for seeing the unemployed.

Lord Caversham on his son, Lord Goring, in *Husband*, act 4.

Cultivated idleness seems to me to be the proper occupation for man.

Letters, 269.
Written to the Editor, *Scots Observer*, on August 13, 1890 in defense of *Dorian Gray*.

𝓘GNORANCE

The sure way of knowing nothing about life is to try to make oneself useful.

Gilbert in "The Critic as Artist," pt. 2, in *Intentions* (1891), repr. in Ellmann, 385.

𝓘MITATION

All imitation in morals and in life is wrong. Through the streets of Jerusalem at the present crawls one who is mad and carries a wooden cross on his shoulders. He is a symbol of the lives that are marred by imitation.

"The Soul of Man," repr. in Ellmann, 266.

*I*MPRESSIONISM

CYRIL: Nature follows the landscape painter then, and takes her effects
from him?

VIVIAN: Certainly. Where, if not from the Impressionists, do we get those
wonderful brown fogs that come creeping down our streets, blurring
the gas-lamps and changing the houses into monstrous shadows? To
whom, if not to them and their master, do we owe the lovely silver mists
that brood over our river, and turn to faint forms of fading grace curved
bridge and swaying barge?

"The Decay of Lying," in *Intentions* (1891), repr. in Ellmann, 312.

In this passage, added to the version published in *Intentions,* Wilde mimics Whistler's "Ten
O'Clock" lecture (1885), which describes the transforming effects "when the evening mist
clothes the riverside with poetry"; indeed, the "master" alluded to here is Whistler.

*I*MPRISONMENT

Not that I am really alone. A slim thing, gold-haired like an angel, stands
always at my side. His presence overshadows me. He moves in the gloom
like a white flower.

Letters, 389.

Written to the parodist and novelist Ada Leverson and Ernest Leverson on Apr. 9, 1895 from
Holloway Prison, concerning Alfred Douglas.

*I*NCREDIBILITY

One should spend one's days in saying what is incredible, and one's
evenings in doing what is improbable.

Quoted in: Small, 129.

*I*NDIFFERENCE

Indifference is the revenge the world takes on mediocrities.

Prince Paul in *Vera,* act 2.

$\mathcal{I}$*NDIVIDUALISM*

He who would lead a Christ-like life is he who is perfectly and absolutely
himself. He may be a great poet, or a great man of science; or a young
student at a University; or one who watches sheep upon a moor; or a
maker of dramas like Shakespeare . . . or a fisherman who throws his nets
into sea. It does not matter what he is, as long as he realizes the perfection
of the soul that is within him.

"The Soul of Man," repr. in Ellmann, 266.

At present, in consequence of the existence of private property, a great
many people are enabled to develop a certain very limited amount of
Individualism. They are either under no necessity to work for their living,
or are enabled to choose the sphere of activity that is really congenial to
them, and gives them pleasure. These are the poets, philosophers, the men
of science, the men of culture—in a word, the real men, the men who have
realised themselves, and in whom all Humanity gains a partial realisation.

"The Soul of Man," repr. in Ellmann, 257.

The new Individualism, for whose service Socialism, whether it wills it or
not, is working, will be perfect harmony. It will be what the Greeks sought
for, but could not, except in Thought, realise completely, because they had
slaves, and fed them. It will be complete, and through it each man will
attain to his perfection. The New Individualism is the new Hellenism.

"The Soul of Man," repr. in Ellmann, 289.

Hellenism, as used by Matthew Arnold, was a cultural ideal derived from ancient Greece,
adapted here by Wilde.

To ask whether Individualism is practical is like asking whether Evolution
is practical. *Evolution is the law of life, and there is no evolution except
towards Individualism.*

"The Soul of Man," repr. in Ellmann, 284-85.

Under Individualism people will be quite natural and absolutely unselfish,
and will know the meanings of the words, and realise them in their free,
beautiful lives. Nor will men be egotistic as they are now. For the egotist is
he who makes claims upon others, and the Individualist will not desire to
do that.

"The Soul of Man," repr. in Ellmann, 285.

INFLUENCE

Dorian Gray had been poisoned by a book. There were moments when he looked on evil simply as a mode through which he could realize his conception of the beautiful.

Dorian Gray, ch. 11.

The poisonous book—according to Wilde—was partly suggested by Joris-Karl Huysmans's *A Rebours* (1884), described at the end of chapter 10 in *Dorian Gray*.

He was dimly conscious that entirely fresh influences were at work within him. Yet they seemed to him to have come really from himself. The few words that Basil's friend had said to him—words spoken by chance, no doubt, and with wilful paradox in them—had touched some secret chord that had never been touched before, but that he felt was now vibrating and throbbing to curious pulses.

Dorian Gray, ch. 2.

Dorian musing on the effect of Lord Henry's influence.

There was something terribly enthralling in the exercise of influence. No other activity was like it. To project one's soul into some form, and let it tarry there for a moment; to hear one's own intellectual views echoed back to one with all the added music of passion and youth; to convey one's temperament into another as though it were a subtle fluid or a strange perfume: there was a real joy in that—perhaps the most satisfying joy left to us in an age so limited and vulgar as our own. . . .

Dorian Gray, ch. 3.

INFORMATION

It is a very sad thing that nowadays there is so little useless information.

"A Few Maxims," repr. in *Letters,* 869.

INJUSTICE

There is only one thing worse than Injustice, and that is Justice without her sword in her hand. When Right is not Might, it is Evil.

Gilbert in "The Critic as Artist," pt. 2, in *Intentions* (1891), repr. in Ellmann, 405.

*I*NSINCERITY

Is insincerity such a terrible thing? I think not. It is merely a method by which we can multiply our personalities.

> *Dorian Gray*, ch. 11.
>
> The third sentence reappears in "The Critic as Artist," pt. 2, repr. in Ellmann, 393.

*I*NTELLECTUAL LIFE

In the development of the intellectual life it is only those who know where they are going that ever lose their way.

> Quoted in: Small, 130.

*I*RELAND

Blue Books are generally dull reading, but Blue Books on Ireland have always been interesting. They form the record of one of the great tragedies of modern Europe. In them England has written down her indictment against herself, and has given to the world the history of her shame. If in the last century she tried to govern Ireland with an insolence that was intensified by race-hatred and religious prejudice, she has sought to rule her in this century with a stupidity that is aggravated by good intentions.

> "Mr. Froude's Blue Book," in *PMG* (April 13, 1889), repr. in Ellmann, 136.
>
> A review of J. A. Froude's *The Two Chiefs of Dunboy*; in England, a "blue book" (so named because of its blue covers) contains official reports to Parliament.

The case of the South in the Civil War was to my mind much like that of Ireland today. It was not a struggle to see the empire dismembered, but only to see the Irish people free, and Ireland still as a willing and integral part of the British Empire. To dismember a great empire in this age of vast armies and overweening ambition on the part of other nations is to consign the peoples of the broken country to weak and insigificant places in the panorama of the nations. . . .

> Quoted in: Lewis and Smith, 366.
>
> In an interview, in June 1882, with a *New Orleans Picayune* reporter.

*I*RISH, THE

We Irish are too poetical to be poets; we are a nation of brilliant failures, but we are the greatest talkers since the Greeks.

Quoted in: "Four Years: 1887-1891," pt. 10, in *The Autobiography of W. B. Yeats* (New York, 1965); slightly different versions occur in Yeats's "Hopes and Fears for Irish Literature," in *United Ireland* (October 15, 1892), repr. in *Uncollected Prose by W. B. Yeats*, ed. John Frayne (New York, 1970), 1:250; and in *Memoirs*, ed. Denis Donoghue (New York, 1973), 22.

*I*RVING, HENRY

Irving's legs are limpid and utter. Both are delicately intellectual, but his left leg is a poem.

Quoted in: Lewis and Smith, 15.

Wilde uses the fashionable vocabulary of Aestheticism, such as "limpid" and "utter," to characterize the actor.

*J*AMES, HENRY

Mr. Henry James writes fiction as if it were a painful duty, and wastes upon mean motives and imperceptible "points of view" his neat literary style, his felicitous phrases, his swift and caustic satire.

Vivian in "The Decay of Lying," in *Intentions* (1891), repr. in Ellmann, 295.

*J*OURNALISM

As for modern journalism, it is not my business to defend it. It justifies its own existence by the great Darwinian principle of the survival of the vulgarest.

Gilbert in "The Critic as Artist," pt. 1, in *Intentions* (1891), repr. in Ellmann, 349.

There is much to be said in favour of modern journalism. By giving us the opinions of the uneducated, it keeps us in touch with the ignorance of the community. By carefully chronicling the current events of contemporary life, it shows us of what very little importance such events really are.

Gilbert in "The Critic as Artist," pt. 2, in *Intentions* (1891), repr. in Ellmann, 393.

Who can help laughing when an ordinary journalist seriously proposes to limit the subject-matter at the disposal of the artist? Some limitation might well, and will soon, I hope, be placed upon some of our newspapers and newspaper writers. For they give us the bald, sordid, disgusting facts of life. They chronicle, with degrading avidity, the sins of the second-rate, and with the conscientiousness of the illiterate give us accurate and prosaic details of the doings of people of absolutely no interest whatsoever.

Gilbert in "The Critic as Artist," pt. 2, in *Intentions* (1891), repr. in Ellmann, 394.

We are dominated by Journalism. In America the President reigns for four years, and Journalism governs for ever and ever.

"The Soul of Man," repr. in Ellmann, 276.

The journalist is always reminding the public of the existence of the artist. That is unnecessary of him. He is always reminding the artist of the existence of the public. That is indecent of him.

Quoted in: Gilbert Burgess's "*An Ideal Husband* at the Haymarket Theater: A Talk with Mr. Oscar Wilde," *Sketch* (January 9, 1895), repr. in Mikhail 1:242.

I never heard that up to that time his only occupation was selling newspapers. It is the first I have heard of his connexion with literature.

Quoted in: Hyde, 121.

Wilde responding to a question concerning a young man whom he had befriended, this response in the April 1895 libel trial involving the Marquess of Queensberry, who had charged Wilde with "posing" as a sodomite.

KEATS, JOHN

Byron was a rebel and Shelley a dreamer; but in the calmness and clearness of his vision, his perfect self-control, his unerring sense of beauty and his recognition of a separate realm for the imagination, Keats was the pure and serene artist, the forerunner of the pre-Raphaelite school, and so of the great romantic movement. . . .

"English Renaissance," pub. in *Miscellanies*, 249.

. . . when Keats died the Muses still had left
One silver voice to sing his threnody,
But ah! too soon of it we were bereft
When on that riven night and stormy sea
Panthea claimed her singer as her own,
And slew the mouth that praised her. . . .

"The Garden of Eros," lines 127-32, in *Poems* (1881), repr. in *Poems* (1997).

The "one silver voice" refers to Shelley, who composed "Adonais," a threnody, or song of
lamentation, eulogizing Keats; Shelley was later drowned; Panthea is an ocean spirit, which
appears in Shelley's *Prometheus Unbound* (1820).

O poet-painter of our English Land!
Thy name was writ in water—it shall stand:
And tears like mine shall keep thy memory green,
As Isabella did her Basil-tree.

"The Grave of Keats," in the *Irish Monthly* (July 1877), repr. in *Poems* (1997).

Written after a visit to the Protestant Cemetery in Rome; "name was writ in water" was Keats's
own epitaph; Keats's poem "Isabella; or, the Pot of Basil," derived from Boccaccio's
Decameron, depicts a woman who hides her murdered lover's head in a pot of basil.

Rid of the world's injustice, and his pain,
He rests at last beneath God's veil of blue:
Taken from life when life and love were new
The youngest of the Martyrs here is lain,
Fair as Sebastian, and as early slain.

"The Grave of Keats," in *Irish Monthly* (July 1877), repr. in *Poems* (1997).

Written after visiting Keats's grave in the Protestant Cemetery in Rome; St. Sebastian was the
favorite saint of late l9th-century homosexuals.

Yet tarry! for the boy who loved thee best,
Whose very name should be a memory
To make thee linger, sleeps in silent rest
Beneath the Roman walls, and melody
Still mourns her sweetest lyre, none can play
The lute of Adonais, with his lips Song passed away.

"The Garden of Eros," lines 121-26, in *Poems* (1881), repr. in *Poems* (1997).

Keats, the "boy" who loved Beauty best, is buried in the Protestant Cemetery in Rome; Shelley
wrote the elegy "Adonais" (1821) on Keats's death; in the following year, Shelley himself died
and was also buried in the Protestant Cemetery.

These are the letters which Endymion wrote
To one he loved in secret, and apart.
And now the brawlers of the auction mart

Bargain and bid for each poor blotted note. . . .
. . . I think they love not Art
Who break the crystal of a poet's heart
That small and sickly eyes may glare and gloat.

"On the Sale by Auction of Keats' Love Letters," in the *Dramatic Review* (January 23, 1886), repr. in *Poems* (1997).

Keats's letters to his beloved Fanny Brawne were written between July 1819 and early August 1820 and auctioned at Sotheby's (London) on March 2, 1885; the mythological Endymion was the subject of one of Keats's poems, here identified with the poet.

As I stood beside the mean grave of this divine boy, I thought of him as of a Priest of Beauty slain before his time; and the vision of Guido's St. Sebastian came before my eyes as I saw him at Genoa, a lovely brown boy, with crisp, clustering hair and red lips, bound by his evil enemies to a tree, and, though pierced by arrows, raising his eyes with divine, impassioned gaze towards the Eternal Beauty of the opening heavens.

"The Tomb of Keats," in *Irish Monthly* (July 1877), repr. in Ellmann, 5.

Keats, "slain before his time," alludes to his presumed death because of adverse criticism of his poetry rather than to tuberculosis; St. Sebastian was the favorite martyred saint of late-Victorian homosexuals.

KINDNESS

One can always be kind to people about whom one cares nothing.

Lord Henry in *Dorian Gray*, ch. 8.

One can always be kind to people about whom one cares nothing. That is why English family life is so pleasant.

Quoted in: Small, 141.

KIPLING, RUDYARD

As one turns over the pages of [Kipling's] *Plain Tales from the Hills*, one feels as if one were seated under a palm-tree reading life by superb flashes of vulgarity. . . . From the point of view of literature Mr. Kipling is a genius who drops his aspirates. From the point of view of life, he is a reporter who knows vulgarity better than any one has ever known it. . . . He is our first authority on the second-rate, and has seen marvellous things through keyholes. . . .

Gilbert in "The Critic as Artist," pt. 2, in *Intentions* (1891), repr. in Ellmann, 402.

KNOWLEDGE

Knowledge would be fatal. It is the uncertainty that charms me. A mist makes things wonderful.

Lord Henry in *Dorian Gray*, ch. 18.

LADY BRACKNELL: I have always been of opinion that a man who desires to get married should know either everything or nothing. Which do you know?

JACK: I know nothing, Lady Bracknell.

LADY BRACKNELL: I am pleased to hear it. I do not approve of anything that tempers with natural ignorance. Ignorance is like a delicate exotic fruit; touch it and the bloom is gone.

Earnest, act 1.

"Know Thyself" was written over the portal of the antique world. Over the portal of the new world, "Be thyself" shall be written. And the message of Christ to man was simply "Be thyself." That is the secret of Christ.

"The Soul of Man," repr. in Ellmann, 263.

"Know thyself" was inscribed in Greek over the entrance of Apollo's temple at Delphi.

LABOR

All unintellectual labour, all monotonous, dull labour that deals with dreadful things, and involves unpleasant conditions, must be done by machinery.

"The Soul of Man," repr. in Ellmann, 269.

LANGTRY, LILLIE

Lily of love, pure and inviolate!
Tower of ivory! red rose of fire!
Thou hast come down our darkness to illume:
For we, close-caught in the wide nets of Fate,
Wearied with waiting for the World's Desire,
Aimlessly wandered in the House of gloom. . . .

"The New Helen," lines 91-96, in *Time: A Monthly Miscellany* (July 1879), repr. in *Poems* (1997).
Wilde celebrating the actress Lillie Langtry.

I would rather have discovered Mrs. Langtry than have discovered America.

Quoted in: the Halifax, Nova Scotia, *Morning Herald* (October 10, 1882), repr. in Mikhail, 1:108.

LANGUAGE

If mendacious only means "what can be mended," mercenary "one who feels for another," and parasite "a kind of umbrella," it is evident that latent, in the very lowest citizen of our community, lie capacities for platform oratory hitherto unsuspected.

"The Child-Philosopher," in *CSR* (April 20, 1887), repr. in Mason, 33.

Discussing Mark Twain's review in *Century Magazine* (April 1887) of Caroline B. LeRow's *English as She is Taught*.

There is no mode of action, no form of emotion, that we do not share with the lower animals. It is only by language that we rise above them, or above each other—by language, which is the parent, and not the child, of thought.

Gilbert in "The Critic as Artist," pt. 1, in *Intentions* (1891), repr. in Ellmann, 359.

The dishonesty of the age has coined the most perfectly dreadful word at present forming our language—"second-hand"—the meaning of which is that the moment you begin to use anything it begins to decrease in value until after six months it is worth nothing. I hope that the word will fall into such complete disuse that when philologists in the future try to discover what it means they shall not be able.

"The Decorative Arts," in O'Brien, 154.

Wilde erred: according to the *Oxford English Dictionary*, the first recorded use of *second-hand* is 1654.

I never quarrel with actions. My one quarrel is with words. That is the reason I hate vulgar realism in literature. The man who could call a spade a spade should be compelled to use one. It is the only thing he is fit for.

Lord Henry in *Dorian Gray*, ch. 17.

Words! Mere words! How terrible they were! How clear, and vivid, and cruel! One could not escape from them. And yet what a subtle magic there was in them! They seemed to be able to give a plastic form to formless things, and to have a music of their own as sweet as that of viol or of lute. Mere words! Was there anything so real as words?

Dorian Gray, ch. 2.

Language is the noblest instrument we have, either for the revealing or the concealing of thought; talk itself is a sort of spiritualised action; and conversation is one of the loveliest of the arts.

"Should Geniuses Meet?" in *CSR* (May 4, 1887), repr. in Mason, 38.

LANGUAGE: GERMAN

MISS PRISM: Your German grammar is on the table. Pray open it at page fifteen. We will repeat yesterday's lesson.
CECILY: But I don't like German. It isn't at all a becoming language. I know perfectly well that I look quite plain after my German lesson.

Earnest, act 2.

From Reading Prison in November 1896, Wilde wrote to Robert Ross: "I am going to take up the study of German: indeed this seems to be the proper place for such a study" (*Letters*, 413).

LAUGHTER

Laughter is not at all a bad beginning for a friendship, and it is far the best ending for one.

Lord Henry in *Dorian Gray*, ch. 1.

LAW

Oh, it is indeed a burning shame that there would be one law for men and another law for women. I think that there should be no law for anybody.

> Quoted in: Gilbert Burgess's "*An Ideal Husband* at the Haymarket Theatre: A Talk with Mr. Oscar Wilde," *Sketch* (January 9, 1895), repr. in Mikhail 1:240–41.

LEGENDS

You know, the truth about the life of a man is not what he does, but the legend which he creates around himself. I have never paraded the streets of London with a lily in my hand; for any caretaker or coachman could do the same. That legend merely indicates the impression that I have made on the masses, and it indicates the nature of my temperament better than what I have (actually) done.

> Quoted in: Jacques Daurelle's "An English Poet in Paris," *Echo de Paris* (December 6, 1891), repr. in Mikhail 1:171.

LIARS

The aim of the liar is simply to charm, to delight, to give pleasure. He is the basis of civilized society, and without him a dinner party, even at the mansions of the great, is as dull as a lecture at the Royal Society. . . .

> Vivian in "The Decay of Lying," in *Intentions* (1891), repr. in Ellmann, 305.

LIFE

Life is terribly deficient in form. Its catastrophes happen in the wrong way and to the wrong people. There is a grotesque horror about its comedies, and its tragedies seem to culminate in farce. One is always wounded when one approaches it. Things last either too long, or not long enough.

> Gilbert in "The Critic as Artist," pt. 2, in *Intentions* (1891), repr. in Ellmann, 375.
>
> An argument similar to that in Wilde's "The Decay of Lying" in *Intentions*.

Life! Life! Don't let us go to life for our fulfillment or our experience. It is a thing narrowed by circumstances, incoherent in its utterance, and without that fine correspondence of form and spirit which is the only thing that can satisfy the artistic and critical temperament.

> Gilbert in "The Critic as Artist," pt. 2, in *Intentions* (1891), repr. in Ellmann, 379-80.

The longer one studies life and literature, the more strongly one feels that behind everything that is wonderful stands the individual, and that it is not the moment that makes the man, but the man who creates the age.

> Gilbert in "The Critic as Artist," pt. 1, in *Intentions* (1891), repr. in Ellmann, 356.

When one looks back upon the life that was so vivid in its emotional intensity, and filled with such fervent moments of ecstasy or of joy, it all seems to be a dream and an illusion.

> Gilbert in "The Critic as Artist," pt. 2, in *Intentions* (1891), repr. in Ellmann, 375.

We have had beautiful and imaginative work in which the visible things of life are transmuted into artistic conventions, and the things Life has not are invented and fashioned for her delight. But wherever we have returned to Life and Nature, our work has always become vulgar, common, and uninteresting.

> Vivian in "The Decay of Lying," in *Intentions* (1891), repr. in Ellmann, 303.
> On the decorative arts.

Certainly, to him Life itself was the first, the greatest, of the arts, and for it all the other arts seemed to be but a preparation. Fashion, by which what is really fantastic becomes for a moment universal, and Dandyism, which, in its own way, is an attempt to assert the absolute modernity of beauty, had, of course, their fascination for him.

> *Dorian Gray*, ch. 11.
> Dorian is, for a time, the embodiment of the ideals of Aestheticism; the remark on the modernity of Dandyism reappears in "A Few Maxims."

Life is a question of nerves, and fibres, and slowly built-up cells in which thought hides itself and passion has its dreams. You may fancy yourself safe and think yourself strong. But a chance tone of colour in a room or a morning sky, a particular perfume that you had once loved and that brings subtle memories with it, a line from a forgotten poem that you had come

across again, a cadence from a piece of music that you had ceased to play—
I tell you, Dorian, that it is on things like these that our lives depend.

> Lord Henry in *Dorian Gray*, ch. 19.

Live! Live the wonderful life that is in you! Let nothing be lost upon you.
Be always searching for new sensations. Be afraid of nothing. . . . A new
Hedonism—that is what our century wants. You might be its visible
symbol.

> Lord Henry to Dorian in *Dorian Gray*, ch. 2.
>
> Echoes here of Walter Pater's "Conclusion" to *Studies in the History of the Renaissance* (1873).

The aim of life is self-development. To realize one's nature perfectly—that
is what each of us is here for.

> Lord Henry in *Dorian Gray*, ch. 2.

You are the type of what the age is searching for, and what it is afraid it has
found. I am so glad that you have never done anything, never carved a
statue, or painted a picture, or produced anything outside of yourself! Life
has been your art. You have set yourself to music. Your days are your
sonnets.

> Lord Henry to Dorian in *Dorian Gray*, ch. 19.
>
> On living life as an art, a central concept of Aestheticism.

DORIAN: Life is a great disappointment.
LADY NARBOROUGH: Ah, my dear, don't tell me that you have exhausted
   Life. When a man says that one knows that Life has exhausted him.

> *Dorian Gray*, ch. 15.

. . . Is it not said
Somewhere in Holy Writ, that every man
Should be contented with that state of life
God calls him to? Why should I change their state,
Or meddle with an all-wise providence,
Which has apportioned that some men should starve
And others surfeit? I did not make the world.

> Duke of Padua in *Duchess*, act 2.

I am not sure that I quite know what Pessimism really means. All I do know is that life cannot be understood without much charity, cannot be lived without much charity. It is love, and not German philosophy, that is the true explanation of this world, whatever may be the explanation of the next.

Lord Goring in *Husband*, act 2.

As regards a comedy, I have lost the mainspring of life and art, *la joie de vivre*; it is dreadful. I have pleasures, and passions, but the joy of life is gone. I am going under: the morgue yawns for me.

Letters, 708.

Written to the Frank Harris, later Wilde's biographer, in February 1898 from France.

At every single moment of one's life one is what one is going to be no less than what one has been. Art is a symbol, because man is a symbol.

Letters, 476.

Written to Alfred Douglas in early 1897 from Reading Prison, partly pub. as *De Profundis* (1905).

My whole life seems ruined by this man. The tower of ivory is assailed by the foul thing.

Letters, 384.

Written to Robert Ross on February 28, 1894, concerning the Marquess of Queensberry's charge of sodomy.

One's real life is so often the life that one does not lead. . . .

"L'Envoi," in Rennell Rodd's *Rose Leaf and Apple Leaf* (Philadelphia, 1882), repr. in *Miscellanies*, 38.

Life is much too important a thing ever to talk seriously about it.

Prince Paul in *Vera*, act 2, repeated by Lord Darlington in *Fan*, act 1.

We should treat all the trivial things of life very seriously, and all the serious things of life with sincere and studied triviality.

Quoted in: "Mr Oscar Wilde on Mr Oscar Wilde: An Interview," *St. James's Gazette* (January 18, 1895), unsigned but probably written by Robert Ross and Wilde; repr. in Mikhail 1:250.

Ross had asked Wilde about the philosophy of the forthcoming production of *Earnest*.

Life without industry is barren, and industry without art is barbarism.

Quoted in: Lewis and Smith, 167.

Responding to a reporter's question in Chicago on February 11, 1882.

LISTENING

One should never listen. To listen is a sign of indifference to one's hearers.

"A Few Maxims," repr. in *Letters*, 870.

LITERATURE

Literature always anticipates life. It does not copy it, but moulds it to its purpose. The nineteenth century, as we know it, is largely an invention of Balzac.

Vivian in "The Decay of Lying," in *Intentions* (1891), repr. in Ellmann, 308-09.

In mentioning Balzac, Wilde recalls the series of novels comprising *La Comédie Humaine*.

The best work in literature is always done by those who do not depend upon it for their daily bread, and the highest form of literature, poetry, brings no wealth to the singer.

Letters, 179.

Written to an unknown correspondent in 1885.

LONDON

London is too full of fogs and—and serious people, Lord Windermere. Whether the fogs produce the serious people or whether the serious produce the fogs, I don't know, but the whole thing rather gets on my nerves. . . .

Mrs. Erlynne in *Fan*, act 4.

LONGFELLOW, HENRY WADSWORTH

Longfellow is a great poet only for those who never read poetry.

Quoted in: Chris Healy's *Confessions of a Journalist* (1904), repr. in Mikhail, 2:384.

LOVE

Even in love it is purely a question for physiology. It has nothing to do with our own will. Young men want to be faithful, and are not; old men want to be faithless, and cannot. . . .

Lord Henry in *Dorian Gray*, ch. 2.

The people who love only once in their lives are really the shallow people. What they call their loyalty, and their fidelity, I call either the lethargy of custom or their lack of imagination.

Lord Henry in *Dorian Gray*, ch. 4.

When one is in love, one always begins by deceiving one's self, and one always ends by deceiving others. That is what the world calls a romance.

Lord Henry in *Dorian Gray*, ch. 4; in *A Woman*, act 3, Lord Illingworth speaks the same lines..

You have killed my love. You used to stir my imagination. Now you don't even stir my curiosity. You simply produce no effect. I loved you because you were marvellous, because you had genius and intellect, because you realized the dreams of great poets and gave shape and substance to the shadows of art.

Dorian to the actress Sibyl Vane in *Dorian Gray*, ch. 7.

Love is the sacrament of life; it sets
Virtue where virtue was not; cleanses men
Of all the vile pollutions of this world;
It is the fire which purges gold from dross,
It is the spring which in some wintry soil
Makes innocence to blossom like a rose.

Guido Ferrante in *Duchess*, act 3.

How evil it is to buy Love, and how evil to sell it! And yet what purple hours one can snatch from that grey slowly-moving thing we call Time! My mouth is twisted with kissing, and I feed on fevers. The Cloister or the Café—there is my future. I tried the Hearth, but it was a failure.

Letters, 828.
Written to Robert Ross on May 14, 1900 from Italy.

I know now how much greater love is than everything else. You have taught me the divine secret of the world.

Letters, 397.

Written to Alfred Douglas in May 1895, when Wilde was released on bail after his first criminal trial.

Love is fed by the imagination, by which we become wiser than we know, better than we feel, nobler than we are: by which we can see Life as a whole: by which, and by which alone, we can understand others in their real as in their ideal relations.

Letters, 445.

Written to Alfred Douglas in early 1897 from Reading Prison, partly pub. as *De Profundis* (1905).

There are only two things in the world of any importance, Love and Art. . . .

Letters, 276.

Written to the journalist Arthur Fish in October 1890.

What a silly thing Love is. . . . It is not half as useful as Logic, for it does not prove anything, and it is always telling one of things that are not going to happen, and making one believe things that are not true. In fact, it is quite unpractical, and, as in this age to be practical is everything, I shall go back to Philosophy and study Metaphysics.

The Student in "The Nightingale and the Rose," pub. in *The Happy Prince*.

Wilde's ironic view of love.

Love is not fashionable any more, the poets have killed it. They wrote so much about it that nobody believed them, and I am not surprised. True love suffers, and is silent.

The Catherine Wheel in "The Remarkable Rocket," pub. in *The Happy Prince*.

Wilde's ironic view of love.

Ah! ah! wherefore didst thou not look at me? If thou hadst looked at me thou hadst loved me. Well I know that you wouldst have loved me, and the mystery of Love is greater than the mystery of Death.

Salome to the decapitated head of Iokanaan in *Salome* (1894).

It is when we are wounded by our own hands, or by the hands of others, that love should come to cure us—else what use is love at all? All sins, except a sin against itself, Love should forgive. All lives, save loveless lives, true Love should pardon. A man's love is like that. It is wider, larger, more human than a woman's.

Sir Robert Chiltern in *Husband*, act 2.

One should always be in love. That is the reason one should never marry.

Lord Illingworth in *A Woman*, act 3.

The Intellectual loves or romantic friendships of the Hellenes, which surprise us to-day, they considered spiritually fruitful, a stimulus to thought and virtue—I mean virtue as it was understood by the ancients and the Renaissance, not virtue in the English sense, which is only caution and hypocrisy.

Quoted in: Charles Ricketts, *Oscar Wilde: Recollections* (1932), ch. 2.

*L*YING

CYRIL: Lying! I should have thought that our politicians kept up that habit. VIVIAN: I assure you that they do not. They never rise beyond the level of misrepresentation, and actually condescend to prove, to discuss, to argue. How different from the temper of the true liar, with his frank, fearless statements, his superb irresponsibility, his healthy, natural disdain of proof of any kind!

"The Decay of Lying," in *Intentions* (1891), repr. in Ellmann, 292.

For Wilde, "lying" is creative; in literature, realism is a devotion to mere facts, revealing the writer's lack of imagination.

False Sphinx! False Sphinx! By reedy Styx old Charon, leaning on his oar, Waits for my coin. Go thou before, and leave me to my Crucifix. . . .

The Sphinx, lines 171-72 (1894), repr. in *Poems* (1997).

In Greek myth, Charon, who ferried the dead across the river Styx in the Underworld, received, as payment, a bronze coin usually placed in the corpse's mouth.

I do not like your lips; they are quite straight, like the lips of a man who has never told a lie. I want you to learn to lie so that your lips may become beautiful and curved like the lips of an antique mask.

Quoted in: Gide, ch. 1.

"Lying," as Wilde argues in "The Decay of Lying" in *Intentions* (1891), is central to the artist's creativity.

MARRIAGE

When people are tied together for life they too often regard manners as a mere superfluity, and courtesy as a thing of no moment; but where the bond can be easily broken, its very fragility makes its strength, and reminds the husband that he should always try to please, and the wife that she should never cease to be charming.

"The American Man," in *CSR* (April 13, 1887), repr. in Ellmann, 62.

Of course married life is merely a habit, a bad habit. But then one regrets the loss even of one's worst habits. Perhaps one regrets them the most. They are such an essential part of one's personality.

Lord Henry in *Dorian Gray*, ch. 19.

The one charm of marriage is that it makes a life of deception absolutely necessary for both parties.

Lord Henry in *Dorian Gray*, ch. 1.

What nonsense people talk about happy marriages! A man can be happy with any woman, as long as he does not love her.

Lord Henry in *Dorian Gray*, ch. 15.

ALGERNON: You don't seem to realize, that in married life three is company and two is none.
JACK: That, my dear young friend, is the theory that the corrupt French Drama has been propounding for the last fifty years.
ALGERNON: Yes; and that the happy English home has proved in half the time.

Earnest, act 1.

JACK: I can produce the hand-bag at any moment. . . . I really think that should satisfy you, Lady Bracknell.
LADY BRACKNELL: Me, sir! What has it to do with me? You can hardly imagine that I and Lord Bracknell would dream of allowing our only daughter—a girl brought up with the utmost care—to marry into a cloak-room, and form an alliance with a parcel?

Earnest, act 1.

Lady Bracknell had urged Jack Worthing to acquire some relations as soon as possible.

More marriages are ruined nowadays by the common sense of the husband than by anything else. How can a woman be expected to be happy with a man who insists on treating her as if she were a perfectly rational being?

Mrs. Allonby in *A Woman*, act 2.

*M*ARRIAGE: PROPOSALS

I have a theory that it is always the women who propose to us, and not we who propose to women. Except, of course, in middle-class life. But then the middle classes are not modern.

Lord Henry in *Dorian Gray*, ch. 6.

*M*ARTYRDOM

I would go to the stake for a sensation and be a sceptic to the last!

Letters, 185.
Written to H. C. Marillier, an acquaintance, in early 1886.

There is something of the martyr about her. Her death has all the pathetic uselessness of martyrdom, all its wasted beauty.

Dorian in *Dorian Gray*, ch. 9.
On Sibyl Vane's suicide.

Yes, I have no doubt we shall win, but the road is long, and red with monstrous martyrdoms.

Letters, 721.
Written to the author and homosexual George Ives in March 1898 from France.

Martyrdom was to me merely a tragic form of scepticism, an attempt to realise by fire what one had failed to do by faith. No man dies for what he knows to be true. Men die for what they want to be true, for what some terror in their hearts tells them is not true.

Mr. W. H., pt. 5, repr. in Ellmann, 219.

$\mathcal{M}$ASTERPIECE

Who am I to tamper with a masterpiece?

Quoted in: Edgar Saltus's *Oscar Wilde: An Idler's Impression* (Chicago, 1917; repr. New York, 1968), repr. in Mikhail, 2:427.

A theater manager had asked Wilde to make changes in *Vera*.

$\mathcal{M}$AUPASSANT, GUY DE

M. Guy de Maupassant, with his keen mordant irony and his hard vivid style, strips life of the few poor rags that still cover her, and shows us foul sore and festering wound. He writes lurid little tragedies in which everybody is ridiculous; bitter comedies at which one cannot laugh for very tears.

Vivian in "The Decay of Lying," in *Intentions* (1891), repr. in Ellmann, 296.

$\mathcal{M}$EDIAEVALISM

To be really mediaeval one should have no body. To be really modern one should have no soul. To be really Greek one should have no clothes.

"A Few Maxims," repr. in *Letters*, 870.

Mediaevalism, with its saints and martyrs, its love of self-torture, its wild passion for wounding itself, its gashing with knives, and its whipping with rods—Mediaevalism is real Christianity, and the mediaeval Christ is the real Christ.

"The Soul of Man," repr. in Ellmann, 287.

$\mathcal{M}$EDIOCRITY

Only mediocrities progress. An artist revolves in a cycle of masterpieces, the first of which is no less perfect than the last.

Letters, 372.

Written to the Editor, *PMG*, on September 22, 1894.

$\mathcal{M}$ELODRAMA

We have the modern English melodrama. The characters in these plays talk on the stage exactly as they would talk off it; they have neither aspirations nor aspirates; they are taken directly from life and reproduce its vulgarity down to the smallest detail. . . . And yet how wearisome the plays are! They do not succeed in producing even that impression of reality at which they aim, and which is their only reason for existing. As a method, realism is a complete failure.

> Vivian in "The Decay of Lying," in *Intentions* (1891), repr. in Ellmann, 303.

$\mathcal{M}$EN AND WOMEN

If the English girl ever met him, she would marry him; and if she married him, she would be happy. For, though he may be rough in manner, and deficient in the picturesque insincerity of romance, yet he is invariably kind and thoughtful, and has succeeded in making his own country the Paradise of Women. This, however, is perhaps the reason why, like Eve, the women are always so anxious to get out of it.

> "The American Man," in *CSR* (April 13, 1887), repr. in Ellmann, 64.
> The final line in the passage is echoed by Lord Illingworth in *A Woman*, act 1.

On the whole, the great success of marriage in the States is due partly to the fact that no American man is ever idle, and partly to the fact that no American wife is considered responsible for the quality of her husband's dinners.

> "The American Man," in *CSR* (April 13, 1887), repr. in Ellmann, 62.

I like men who have a future and women who have a past.

> Lord Henry in *Dorian Gray*, ch. 15.

No woman is a genius. Women are a decorative sex. They never have anything to say, but they say it charmingly. Women represent the triumph of matter over mind, just as men represent the triumph of mind over morals.

> Lord Henry in *Dorian Gray*, ch. 4; the passage (beginning with "Women represent . . .") reappears as Lord Illingworth's lines in *A Woman*, act 3.

Men marry because they are tired; women, because they are curious: both are disappointed.

Lord Henry in *Dorian Gray*, ch. 4; in *A Woman*, act 3, Lord Illingworth speaks the same lines.

The only way a woman can ever reform a man is by boring him so completely that he loses all possible interest in life.

Lord Henry in *Dorian Gray*, ch. 8.

Dear Christ! how little pity
We women get in this untimely world;
Men lure us to some dreadful precipice,
And, when we fall, they leave us.

Duchess in *Duchess*, act 3.

I see when men love women
They give them but a little of their lives,
But women when they love give everything.

Duchess in *Duchess*, act 3.

When a man loves a woman, then he knows
God's secret, and the secret of the world.

Guido Ferrante in *Duchess*, act 3.

JACK: You don't think there is any chance of Gwendolen becoming like her mother in about a hundred and fifty years, do you Algy?
ALGERNON: All women become like their mothers. That is their tragedy. No man does. That's his.
JACK: Is that clever?
ALGERNON: It is perfectly phrased! and quite as true as any observation in civilized life should be.

Earnest, act 1; Algernon's first speech had previously appeared in *A Woman*, act 2.

A man who moralizes is usually a hypocrite, and a woman who moralizes is invariably plain. There is nothing in the whole world so unbecoming to a woman as a Nonconformist conscience.

Cecil Graham in *Fan*, act 3.

Between men and women there is no friendship possible. There is passion, enmity, worship, love, but no friendship.

Lord Darlington in *Fan*, act 2.

If a woman wants to hold a man, she has merely to appeal to what is worst in him. We make gods of men and they leave us. Others make brutes of them and they fawn and are faithful. How hideous life is!

Lady Windermere in *Fan*, act 3.

There's nothing in the world like the devotion of a married woman. It's a thing no married man knows anything about.

Cecil Graham in *Fan*, act 3.

Most women are so artificial that they have no sense of Art. Most men are so natural that they have no sense of Beauty.

"A Few Maxims," repr. in *Letters*, 869.

A man's life is of more value than a woman's. It has larger issues, wider scope, greater ambitions. Our lives revolve in curves of emotions. It is upon lines of intellect that a man's life progresses.

Lady Chiltern in *Husband*, act 4.

The strength of women comes from the fact that psychology cannot explain us. Men can be analyzed, women . . . merely adored.

Mrs. Cheveley in *Husband*, act 1.

MRS. MARCHMONT: . . . as far as [Mrs. Cheveley] could see, London Society was entirely made up of dowdies and dandies.
LORD GORING: She is quite right, too. The men are all dowdies and the women are all dandies, aren't they?

Husband, act 1.

Why can't you women love us, faults and all? Why do you place us on monstrous pedestals? We have all feet of clay, women as well as men; but when we men love women, we love them knowing their weaknesses, their follies, their imperfections, love them all the more, it may be, for that reason. It is not the perfect, but the imperfect, who have need of love.

Sir Robert Chiltern in *Husband*, act 2.

If a man and woman have sinned, let them both go forth into the desert to love or loathe each other there. Let them both be branded. Set a mark, if you wish, on each, but don't punish the one and let the other go free. Don't have one law for men and another for women.

Hester Worsley in *A Woman*, act 2.

In the comic context of *Earnest*, act 3, Jack Worthing echoes Hester's final line above.

The Ideal Man should talk to us as if we were goddesses, and treat us as if we were children. He should refuse all our serious requests, and gratify every one of our whims. He should encourage us to have caprices, and forbid us to have missions. He should always say much more than he means, and always mean much more than he says.

Mrs. Allonby in *A Woman*, act 2.

LADY STUTFIELD: Ah! The world was made for men and not for women.
MRS. ALLONBY: Oh, don't say that, Lady Stutfield. We have a much better time than they have. There are far more things forbidden to us than are forbidden to them.

A Woman, act 1.

LORD ILLINGWORTH: The Book of Life begins with a man and a woman in a garden.
MRS. ALLONBY: It ends with Revelations.

A Woman, act 1.

Man, poor, awkward, reliable, necessary man belongs to a sex that has been rational for millions of years. He can't help himself. It is in his race. The History of Woman is very different. We have always been picturesque protests against the mere existence of common sense. We saw its dangers from the first.

Mrs. Allonby in *A Woman*, act 2.

Men always want to be a woman's first love. That is their clumsy vanity. We women have a more subtle instinct about things. What we like is to be a man's last romance.

Mrs. Allonby in *A Woman*, act 2.

When a woman marries again, it is because she detested her first husband. When a man marries again, it is because he adored his first wife. Women try their luck; men risk theirs.

Lord Henry in *Dorian Gray*, ch. 15.

*M*EN

There are two kinds of men in the world, two great creeds, two different forms of natures: men to whom the end of life is action, and men to whom the end of life is thought.

"English Renaissance," pub. in *Miscellanies*, 274.

*M*EN: *AMERICAN*

The ruin and decay of Time has no pathos in his eyes. He turns away from Ravenna, because the grass grows in her streets, and can see no loveliness in Verona, because there is rust on her balconies. His one desire to get the whole of Europe into thorough repair.

"The American Man," in *CSR* (April 13, 1887), repr. in Ellmann, 60.

Their education is quite different from ours. They know men much better than they know books, and life interests them more than literature. They have no time to study anything but the stock markets, no leisure to read anything but newspapers.

"The American Man," in *CSR* (April 13, 1887), repr. in Ellmann, 61.

*M*EREDITH, *GEORGE*

Ah! Meredith! Who can define him? His style is chaos illumined by flashes of lightning. As a writer he has mastered everything except language: as a novelist he can do everything, except tell a story: as an artist he is everything, except articulate.

Vivian in "The Decay of Lying," in *Intentions* (1891), repr. in Ellmann, 298.

MICHELANGELO

One production of Michael Angelo is worth a hundred by Edison.

Quoted in: Lewis and Smith, 167.

Responding to reporters' questions in Chicago on February 11, 1882.

MILTON, JOHN

... where is the pen
Of austere Milton? where the mighty sword
Which slew its master righteously? the years
Have lost their ancient leader, and no word
Breaks from the voiceless tripod on our ears. . . .

"Humanitad," lines 307-10, in *Poems* (1881), repr. in *Poems* (1997).

The "mighty sword" (a metaphorical pen) refers to Milton's *Tenure of Kings and Magistrates* (1649), which argued that a nation's subjects may depose and execute an unjust king; the "tripod" refers to ancient Greek oracles speaking from flaming tripods.

Milton! I think thy spirit hath passed away
From these white cliffs, and high-embattled towers;
This gorgeous fiery-coloured world of ours
Seems fallen into ashes dull and grey. . . .

"To Milton," in *Poems* (1881), repr. in *Poems* (1997).

Wilde modeled his sonnet after Wordsworth's "London 1802": "Milton! Thou shouldst be living at this hour," also concerned with England's moral decline.

MIRACLES

It is difficult to shake the popular belief in miracles, but no man will admit sin and immorality as attributes of the ideal he worships. . . .

"Historical Criticism," pt. 2.

It is not for Him that I am weeping, but for myself. I too have changed water into wine, and I have healed the leper and given sight to the blind. I have walked upon the waters, and from the dwellers in the tombs I have

cast out devils . . . and I have raised the dead from their narrow houses. . . .
All things that this man has done I have done also. And yet they have not
crucified me.

"The Master," in the *FR* (July 1894), repr. in *Poems* (1997).

A young man, naked and weeping, responds to Joseph of Arimathea's remark: "I do not wonder
that your sorrow is so great, for surely He was a just man."

Miracles always happen. That is why one cannot believe in them.

Quoted in: Small, 130.

*M*ISFORTUNE

Misfortunes one can endure—they come from outside, they are accidents.
But to suffer for one's own faults—ah!—there is the sting of life.

Lord Windermere in *Fan*, act 1.

*M*ISSIONARIES

Don't you realize that missionaries are the divinely provided food for
destitute and under-fed cannibals? Whenever they are on the brink of
starvation, Heaven, in its infinite mercy, sends them a nice plump
missionary.

Quoted in: Richard Le Gallienne's *The Romantic '90s* (1926), ch. 5; repr. in Mikhail, 2:391.

A remark directed at Mrs. Oscar Wilde, interested in the work of missionaries.

*M*ODERATION

Moderation is a fatal thing. Enough is as bad as a meal. More than enough
is as good as a feast.

Lord Henry in *Dorian Gray*, ch. 15.

LADY HUNSTANTON: Women should think in moderation, as they should
do all things in moderation.

LORD ILLINGWORTH: Moderation is a fatal thing, Lady Hunstanton.
Nothing succeeds like excess.

A Woman, act 3.

Modern times

To realize the nineteenth century, one must realize every century that has
preceded it and that has contributed to its making. To know anything
about oneself, one must know all about others. There must be no mood
with which one cannot sympathize, no dead mode of life that one cannot
make alive.

Gilbert in "The Critic as Artist," pt. 2, in *Intentions* (1891), repr. in Ellmann, 382.

Nothing is so dangerous as being too modern. One is apt to grow old-
fashioned quite suddenly.

Lady Markby in *Husband*, act 2.

The nineteenth century may be a prosaic age, but we fear that, if we are to
judge by the general run of novels, it is not an age of prose.

"One of Mr. Conway's Remainders," in *PMG* (February 1, 1886), repr. in *Reviews*, 42.

A review of Hugh Conway's *A Cardinal Sin.*

Modernity

Modernity of form and modernity of subject-matter are entirely and
absolutely wrong. We have mistaken the common livery of the age for the
vesture of the Muses, and spend our days in the sordid streets and hideous
suburbs of our vile cities when we should be out on the hillside with
Apollo. Certainly we are a degraded race, and have sold our birthright for a
mess of facts.

Vivian in "The Decay of Lying," in in *Intentions* (1891), repr. in Ellmann, 300.

In the final sentence, Wilde echoes the story of Esau, who has sold his birthright for a mess of
pottage (Genesis 25).

To be modern is the only thing worth being nowadays. . . . A man who can
dominate a London dinner-table can dominate the world. The future
belongs to the dandy. It is the exquisites who are going to rule.

Lord Illingworth in *A Woman*, act 3.

$\mathcal{M}$ONEY

LORD FERMOR: Young people, nowadays, imagine that money is
everything.
LORD HENRY: Yes, and when they grow older they know it.

Dorian Gray, ch. 3.

The only thing that can console one for having no money is extravagance.

Quoted in: Small, 141.

$\mathcal{M}$OON, THE

The moon has a strange look tonight. Has she not a strange look? She is
like a mad woman, a mad woman who is seeking everywhere for lovers.
She is naked too. She is quite naked. The clouds are seeking to clothe her
nakedness, but she will not let them. She shows herself naked in the sky.

Herod in *Salome* (1894).

The implied analogy is between the moon and Salome.

$\mathcal{M}$OORE, GEORGE

George Moore has conducted his whole education in public. He had
written two or three books before he found out there was such a thing as
English grammar.

Quoted in: Harris, ch. 23.

Moore, the Irish novelist, was not one of Wilde's circle.

$\mathcal{M}$ORAL

The moral is this: All excess, as well as all renunciation, brings its own
punishment.

Letters, 259.

Written to the Editor, *St. James's Gazette* on June 26, 1890 in defense of *Dorian Gray*.

Yes; there is a terrible moral in *Dorian Gray*—a moral which the prurient will not be able to find in it, but which will be revealed to all whose minds are healthy. Is this an artistic error? I fear it is. It is the only error in the book.

Letters, 259.

Written to the Editor, *St. James's Gazette* on June 26, 1890 in defense of *Dorian Gray*.

*M*ORALISTS

Moralists spend their lives in warning people against the sins of which they have grown tired. The active moralist is a tired Hedonist. At least, he should be.

Quoted in: Small, 141.

*M*ORALITY

Modern morality consists in accepting the standard of one's age. I consider that for any man of culture to accept the standard of his age is a form of the grossest immorality.

Lord Henry in *Dorian Gray*, ch. 6.

BASIL HALLWARD: You never say a moral thing, and you never do a wrong thing. Your cynicism is simply a pose.
LORD HENRY: Being natural is simply a pose, and the most irritating pose I know.

Dorian Gray, ch. 1.

Morality is simply the attitude we adopt towards people whom we personally dislike.

Mrs. Cheveley in *Husband*, act 2.

Moral people, as they are termed, are simple beasts. I would sooner have fifty unnatural vices than one unnatural virtue. It is unnatural virtue that makes the world, for those who suffer, such a premature Hell.

Letters, 686.

Written to the publisher Leonard Smithers in November 1897 from Italy.

$\mathcal{M}$ORBIDITY

MRS. MARCHMONT: Marchmont and I have been married for seven years, and he has never once told me that I was morbid. Men are so painfully unobservant!

LADY BASILDON: I have always said, dear Margaret, that you were the most morbid person in London.

MRS. MARCHMONT: Ah! but you are always sympathetic, Olivia!

Husband, act 1.

$\mathcal{M}$ORRIS, WILLIAM

I have always felt that your work comes from the sheer delight of making beautiful things: that no alien motive ever interests you: that in its singleness of aim, as well as in its perfection of result, it is pure art, everything that you do.

Letters, 291.

Written to the poet and Socialist in early 1891.

Of all our modern poets Mr. William Morris is the one best qualified by nature and by art to translate for us the marvellous epic of the wanderings of Odysseus. . . . Master as he is of decorative and descriptive verse, he has all the Greek's joy in the visible aspect of things, all the Greek's sense of delicate and delightful detail, all the Greek's pleasure in beautiful textures, and exquisite materials, and imaginative designs. . . .

"William Morris's Odyssey," in *PMG* (April 26, 1887), repr. in Ellmann, 73.

$\mathcal{M}$OURNING

Mourn for Ophelia, if you like. Put ashes on your head because Cordelia was strangled. Cry out against Heaven because the daughter of Brabantio died. But don't waste your tears over Sibyl Vane. She was less real than they are.

Lord Henry to Dorian in *Dorian Gray*, ch. 8.

On Sibyl Vane, who perhaps performed in the various roles mentioned here (Wilde errs: in *King Lear*, Cordelia is not strangled but hanged).

Well, I don't like your clothes. You look perfectly ridiculous in them. Why on earth don't you go up and change? It is perfectly childish to be in deep mourning for a man who is actually staying for a whole week in your house as a guest. I call it grotesque.

> Algernon Moncrieff in *Earnest*, act 2.

> Jack Worthing has been wearing mourning clothes over the death of his imaginary brother, Ernest, whose identity Algernon has assumed.

*M*URDER

O damned saint? O angel fresh from Hell!
What bloody devil tempted thee to this!
That thou hast killed thy husband, that is nothing—
Hell was already gaping for his soul—
But thou hast murdered Love, and in its place
Has set a horrible and bloodstained thing. . . .

> Guido Ferrante in *Duchess*, act 3.

> His reaction to the Duchess's murder of her husband.

Some love too little, some too long,
Some sell, and others buy;
Some do the deed with many tears,
And some without a sigh:
For each man kills the thing he loves,
Yet each man does not die.

> *Reading Gaol*, lines 49-54, repr. in *Poems* (1997).

The man had killed the thing he loved,
And so he had to die.
Yet each man kills the thing he loves,
By each let this be heard,
Some do it with a bitter look,
Some with a flattering word,
The coward does it with a kiss,
The brave man with a sword!

> *Reading Gaol*, lines 35-42, repr. in *Poems* (1997).

> Alludes to the trooper, who had killed his wife out of jealousy.

$\mathcal{M}$USIC

ALGERNON: You see, if one plays good music, people don't listen, and if one plays bad music people don't talk. . . .

LADY BRACKNELL: . . . I'm sure the programme will be delightful, after a few expurgations. French songs I cannot possibly allow. People always seem to think they are improper, and either look shocked, which is vulgar, or laugh, which is worse. But German sounds a thoroughly respectable language, and indeed, I believe is so.

Earnest, act 1.

Then suddenly the tune went false,
The dancers wearied of the waltz,
The shadows ceased to wheel and whirl,
And down the long and silent street,
The dawn with silver-sandalled feet,
Crept like a frightened girl.

"The Harlot's House," in the *Dramatic Review* (April 11, 1885), repr. in *Poems* (1997).

Music is the art in which form and matter are always one—the art whose subject cannot be separated from the method of its expression; the art which most completely realises for us the artistic ideal, and is the condition to which all the other arts are constantly aspiring.

"L'Envoi," in Rennell Rodd's *Rose Leaf and Apple Leaf* (Philadelphia, 1882), repr. in *Miscellanies*, 31.

Wilde echoes Walter Pater's "The School of Giorgione," in *FR* (October 1877), repr. in *The Renaissance* (3rd. ed., 1888): "All art constantly aspires towards the condition of music."

$\mathcal{M}$YSTERY

The true mystery of the world is the visible, not the invisible.

Lord Henry in *Dorian Gray*, ch. 2.

$\mathcal{N}$AMES

ALGERNON: . . . your name isn't Jack at all; it is Ernest.

JACK: It isn't Ernest; it's Jack.

ALGERNON: You have always told me it was Ernest. I have introduced you to everyone as Ernest. You answer to the name of Ernest. You look as if your name was Ernest. You are the most earnest looking person I ever saw in my life.

Earnest, act 1.

JACK: But you don't mean to say that you couldn't love me if my name wasn't Ernest?

GWENDOLEN: But your name is Ernest.

JACK: ... But supposing it was something else? Do you mean to say you couldn't love me then?

GWENDOLEN: Ah! that is clearly a metaphysical speculation, and like most metaphysical speculations has very little reference at all to the actual facts of real life, as we know them.

Earnest, act 1.

$\mathcal{N}$ARCISSISM

I wish I could love. But I seem to have lost the passion, and forgotten the desire. I am too much concentrated on myself. My own personality has become a burden to me.

Dorian in *Dorian Gray*, ch. 18.

I loved Narcissus because, as he lay on my banks and looked down at me, in the mirror of his eyes I saw ever my own beauty mirrored.

"The Disciple," in *Spirit Lamp* (June 6, 1893), repr. in *Poems* (1997).

The reflecting pool speaks to the Oreads, nymphs of the mountains.

"Narcissuses of imbecility," what should they see in the clear waters of Beauty and in the well undefiled of Truth but the shifting and shadowy image of their own substantial stupidity?

Letters, 98-99.

Written to the writer Joaquin Miller on February 26, 1882 concerning the negative comments by the author T. W. Higginson concerning Wilde's poetry.

I am not going to stop talking to [the Frog] merely because he pays no attention. I like hearing myself talk. It is one of my greatest pleasures. I

often have long conversations all by myself, and I am so clever that
sometimes I don't understand a single word of what I am saying.

The Rocket in "The Remarkable Rocket," pub. in *The Happy Prince.*

The only thing that sustains one through life is the consciousness of the
immense inferiority of everybody else. . . .

The Rocket in "The Remarkable Rocket," pub. in *The Happy Prince.*

MRS ALLONBY: . . . what have you been doing lately that astonishes you?
LORD ILLINGWORTH: I have been discovering all kinds of beautiful qualities
in my own nature.

A Woman, act 3.

To love oneself is the beginning of a life-long romance.

"Phrases and Philosophies," repr. in Ellmann, 434; the aphorism reappears in Lord Goring's opening
lines in *Husband,* act 3.

Nature

Nature is so uncomfortable. Grass is hard and lumpy and damp, and full of
dreadful black insects. Why, even [William] Morris's poorest workman
could make you a more comfortable seat than the whole of Nature can.

Vivian in "The Decay of Lying," in *Intentions* (1891), repr. in Ellmann, 291.

And then Nature is so indifferent, so unappreciative. Whenever I am
walking in the park here, I always feel that I am no more to her than the
cattle that browse on the slope, or the burdock that blooms in the ditch.

Vivian in "The Decay of Lying," in *Intentions* (1891), repr. in Ellmann, 291.

If Nature had been comfortable, mankind would never have invented
architecture, and I prefer houses to the open air. In a house we all feel of
the proper proportions. Everything is subordinated to us, fashioned for our
use and our pleasure.

Vivian in "The Decay of Lying," in *Intentions* (1891), repr. in Ellmann, 291.

Nature is no great mother who has borne us. She is our creation. It is in our brain that she quickens to life. Things are because we see them, and what we see, and how we see it, depends on the Arts that have influenced us.

Vivian in "The Decay of Lying," in *Intentions* (1891), repr. in Ellmann, 312.

Nothing is more evident than that Nature hates Mind. Thinking is the most unhealthy thing in the world, and people die of it just as they die of any other disease. Fortunately, in England at any rate, thought is not catching.

Vivian in "The Decay of Lying," in *Intentions* (1891), repr. in Ellmann, 291.

One touch of Nature may make the whole world kin, but two touches of Nature will destroy any work of Art. If, on the other hand, we regard Nature as the collection of phenomena external to man, people only discover in her what they bring to her. . . . Wordsworth went to the lakes, but he was never a lake poet. He found in stones the sermons he had already hidden there. He went moralizing about the district, but his good work was produced when he returned, not to Nature but to poetry.

Vivian in "The Decay of Lying," in *Intentions* (1891), repr. in Ellmann, 300-01.

"Sermons in stones" is Shakespeare's phrase in *As You Like It*, act 2, sc. 1.

A thing in Nature becomes much lovelier if it reminds us of a thing in Art, but a thing in Art gains no real beauty through reminding us of a thing in Nature. The primary aesthetic impression of a work of art borrows nothing from recognition or resemblance.

Letters, 301.

Written to the Editor, *Speaker*, in December 1891, on the decorative designs of *A House of Pomegranates* (1891).

I had no joy in Nature; what to me,
Ambition's slave, was crimson-stained rose,
Or the gold-sceptred crocus? The bright bird
Sang out of tune for me, and the sweet flowers
Seemed but a pageant, and an unreal show
That mocked my heart. . . .

"Sen Artysty; or, The Artist's Dream," lines 22-27, in Clement Scott, ed., *Routledge's Christmas Annual: The Green Room* (1880), repr. in *Poems* (1997).

This translation from Polish of a poem by the actress Helena Modjeska was no doubt Wilde's revision of her own translation since he knew no Polish; the attitude towards nature was characteristic of French Decadence, which stressed artifice in art and life.

New York

Though one can dine in New York one could not dwell there. Better the Far West, with its grizzly bears and its untamed cowboys, its free, open-air and its free, open-air manners, its boundless prairie and its boundless mendacity!

"The American Invasion," *CSR* (March 23, 1887), repr. in Ellmann, 54.

Niagara Falls

I was disappointed with Niagara—most people must be disappointed with Niagara. Every American bride is taken there, and the sight of the stupendous waterfall must be one of the earliest, if not the keenest, disappointments in American married life.

Impressions of America, ed. Stuart Mason (Sunderland, 1906), repr. in Ellmann, 7.

When I first saw Niagara Falls, I was disappointed in the outline. The design, it seemed to me, was wanting in grandeur and variety of line, but the colors were beautiful. . . . The sight was far beyond what I had ever seen in Europe. It seems a sort of embodiment of Pantheism. I thought of what Leonardo da Vinci said once, that the two most wonderful things in the world are a woman's smile and the motion of mighty waters.

Quoted in: Lewis and Smith, 163.

As reported in 1882 in the *Niagara Falls Gazette*.

Night

Out of the unreal shadows of the night comes back the real life that we had known. We have to resume it where we had left off, and there steals over us a terrible sense of the necessity for the continuance of energy in the same wearisome round of stereotyped habits, or a wild longing, it may be, that our eyelids might open some morning upon a world that had been refashioned anew in the darkness for our pleasure. . . .

Dorian Gray, ch. 11.

Again, Wilde puns on his name.

NIGHTINGALE

... in the almond-scented vale
The lonely nightingale is heard.
The day will make thee silent soon,
O nightingale sing on for love!
While yet upon the shadowy grove
Splinter the arrows of the moon.

"By the Arno," in *Dublin University Magazine* (March 1876), repr. in *Poems* (1997).

The male nightingale, the Romantic poets' favorite bird, sings only during the breeding season.

NONSENSE

ALGERNON: I love scrapes. They are the only things that are never serious.
JACK: Oh, that's nonsense, Algy. You never talk anything but nonsense.
ALGERNON: Nobody ever does.

Earnest, act 1.

OBJECTIVITY

The more objective a creation appears to be, the more subjective it really is. Shakespeare might have met Rosencrantz and Guildenstern in the white streets of London ... but Hamlet came out of his soul, and Romeo out of his passion. They were elements of his nature to which he gave visible form, impulses that stirred so strongly within him that he had, as it were perforce, to suffer them to realize their energy. ...

Gilbert in "The Critic as Artist," pt. 2, in *Intentions* (1891), repr. in Ellmann, 389.

OCCUPATIONS

LADY BRACKNELL: Do you smoke?
JACK: Well, yes, I must admit I smoke.

LADY BRACKNELL: I am glad to hear it. A man should always have an occupation of some kind. There are far too many idle men in London as it is.

Earnest, act 1.

Old age

How sad it is! I shall grow old, and horrible, and dreadful. But this picture will remain always young. It will never be older than this particular day of June.... If it were only the other way! If it were I who was to be always young, and the picture that was to grow old! For that—for that—I would give everything! Yes, there is nothing in the whole world I would not give! I would give my soul for that!

Dorian in *Dorian Gray*, ch. 2.
Echoes the Faust legend.

The old believe everything: the middle-aged suspect everything: the young know everything.

"Phrases and Philosophies," repr. in Ellmann, 434.

I delight in men over seventy. They always offer one the devotion of a lifetime.

Mrs. Allonby in *A Woman*, act 4.

Opinions

Public opinion exists only where there are no ideas.

"A Few Maxims," repr. in *Letters*, 869.

Optimism

SIR ROBERT CHILTERN: ... may I ask, at heart, are you an optimist or a pessimist? Those seem to be the only two fashionable religions left to us nowadays.

MRS. CHEVELEY: Oh, I'm neither. Optimism begins in a broad grin, and
Pessimism ends with blue spectacles. Besides, they are both of them
merely poses.

Husband, act 1.

The blue spectacles presumably worn to protect one's eyes against the glare of reality.

People who count their chickens before they are hatched act very wisely:
because chickens run about so absurdly that it is almost impossible to
count them accurately. . . .

Letters, 749.

Written to Robert Ross on May 31, 1898 from France.

ORIGINS

Mr. Worthing, is Miss Cardew at all connected with any of the larger
railway stations in London? I merely desire information. Until yesterday I
had no idea that there were any families or persons whose origin was a
Terminus.

Lady Bracknell in *Earnest*, act 3.

Her query resulting from Jack's story that he had been found in a handbag in the Victoria
Station, the Brighton line.

OXFORD UNIVERSITY

The two great turning-points of my life were when my father sent me to
Oxford, and when society sent me to prison. . . . I was so typical a child of
my age that in my perversity, and for that perversity's sake, I turned the
good things of my life to evil, and the evil things of my life to good.

Letters, 469.

Written to Alfred Douglas in early 1897 from Reading Prison, partly pub. as *De Profundis*
(1905).

PAIN

Pain, if it comes, cannot last for ever; surely one day you and I will meet
again, and though my face be a mask of grief and my body worn out by

solitude, you and you alone will recognize the soul which is more beautiful for having met yours, the soul of the artist who found his ideal in you, of the lover of beauty to whom you appeared as a being flawless and perfect. . . .

Letters, 397.

Written to Alfred Douglas in May 1895, when Wilde was released on bail after his first criminal trial.

*P*AINTERS

I am very fond of the work of many of the Impressionist painters of Paris and London. Subtlety and distinction have not yet left the school. Some of their arrangements and harmonies serve to remind one of the unapproachable beauty of Gautier's immortal *Symphonie en Blanc Majeur*, that flawless masterpiece of colour and music which may have suggested the type as well as the titles of many of their best pictures.

Gilbert in "The Critic as Artist," pt. 2, in *Intentions* (1891), repr. in Ellmann, 397.

Whistler had titled many of his paintings "arrangements," "symphonies," and "harmonies."

The painter is so far limited that it is only through the mask of the body that he can show us the mystery of the soul; only through conventional images that he can handle ideas; only through its physical equivalents that he can deal with psychology.

Gilbert in "The Critic as Artist," pt. 1, in *Intentions* (1891), repr. in Ellmann, 369.

*P*AINTING

His work was that curious mixture of bad painting and good intentions that always entitles a man to be called a representative British artist.

Lord Henry in *Dorian Gray*, ch. 19.

Lord Henry's estimate of Basil Hallward's work since Dorian's portrait.

*P*ANTHEISM

. . . we two lovers shall not sit afar,
Critics of nature, but the joyous sea
Shall be our raiment, and the bearded star

Shoot arrows at our pleasure! We shall be
Part of the mighty universal whole,
And through all aeons mix and mingle with the Kosmic Soul!

"Panthea," lines 169-74, in *Poems* (1881), repr. in *Poems* (1997).

We shall be notes in that great Symphony
Whose cadence circles through the rhythmic spheres,
And all the live World's throbbing heart shall be
One with our heart, the stealthy creeping years
Have lost their terrors now, we shall not die,
The Universe itself shall be our Immortality!

"Panthea," lines 175-80, in *Poems* (1881), repr. in *Poems* (1997).

*P*APACY AND POPES

To the wickedness of the Papacy humanity owes much. The goodness of
the Papacy owes a terrible debt to humanity. Yet, though the Vatican has
kept the rhetoric of its thunders and lost the rod of its lightning, it is better
for the artist not to live with Popes.

"The Soul of Man," repr. in Ellmann, 282-83.

*P*ARADOX

Paradox though it may seem—and paradoxes are always dangerous
things—it is none the less true that Life imitates art far more than Art
imitates life. . . . A great artist invents a type, and Life tries to copy it, to
reproduce it in a popular form, like an enterprising publisher.

Vivian in "The Decay of Lying," in *Intentions* (1891), repr. in Ellmann, 307.

The way of paradoxes is the way of truth. To test Reality we must see it on
the tight rope. When the Verities become acrobats, we can judge them.

Mr. Erskine in *Dorian Gray*, ch. 3.

DUCHESS OF MONMOUTH: Then what should we call you, Harry?
DORIAN: His name is Prince Paradox.
DUCHESS: I recognize him in a flash.

LORD HENRY: I won't hear of it. From a label there is no escape! I refuse the
title.

Dorian Gray, ch. 17.

PARENTS

Few parents nowadays pay any regard to what their children say to them.
The old-fashioned respect for the young is fast dying out.

Gwendolen Fairfax in *Earnest*, act 1.

LADY BRACKNELL: Now to minor matters. Are your parents living?
JACK: I have lost both my parents.
LADY BRACKNELL: Both? To lose one parent may be regarded as a
misfortune—to lose *both* seems like carelessness.

Earnest, act 1.

PARODY

Parodies are a legitimate form of art . . . but the art that appeals to laughter
and the art that appeals to beauty are different things.

Letters, 174.
Written to Edwin Pamler, Editor, *Dramatic Review*, in early 1885.

Parody, which is the Muse with her tongue in her cheek, has always amused
me; but it requires a light touch, a fanciful treatment, and, oddly enough, a
love of the poet whom it caricatures.

More Letters, 81.
Written to the writer Walter Hamilton in January 1889.

PASSION

To note the curious hard logic of passion, and the emotional coloured life
of the intellect—to observe where they met, and where they separated, at
what point they were in union, and at what point they were at discord—

there was a delight in that! What matter what the cost was? One could never pay too high a price for any sensation.

Dorian Gray, ch. 4.

Lord Henry on the complexities of human life.

To drift with every passion till my soul
Is a stringed lute on which all winds can play,
Is it for this that I have given away
Mine ancient wisdom, and austere control?

"Hélas!" in *Poems* (1881), repr. in *Poems* (1997).

This poem was printed in italics as the introductory sonnet to *Poems*, presumably intended as Wilde's credo, which questions the value of a life devoted to mere sensations.

PAST, THE

The one charm of the past is that it is the past. But women never know when the curtain has fallen. They always want a sixth act, and as soon as the interest of the play is entirely over they propose to continue it. If they were allowed their own way, every comedy would have a tragic ending, and every tragedy would culminate in a farce.

Lord Henry in *Dorian Gray*, ch. 8.

The past could always be annihilated. Regret, denial, or forgetfulness could do that. But the future was inevitable. There were passions in him that would find their terrible outlet, dreams that would make the shadow of their evil real.

Dorian Gray, ch. 10.

PATER, WALTER

Even the work of Mr. Pater, who is, on the whole, the most perfect master of English prose now creating amongst us, is often far more like a piece of mosaic than a passage in music, and seems, here and there, to lack the true rhythmical life of words and the fine freedom and richness of effect that such rhythmical life produces.

Gilbert in "The Critic as Artist," pt. 1, in *Intentions* (1891), repr. in Ellmann, 351.

Who, again, cares whether Mr. Pater has put into the portrait of Mona Lisa something Lionardo never dreamed of? . . . And so the picture becomes more wonderful to us than it really is, and reveals to us a secret of which, in truth, it knows nothing. . . . And it is for this very reason that the criticism which I have quoted is criticism of the highest kind. It treats the work of art simply as a starting-point for a new creation. It does not confine itself . . . to discovering the real intention of the artist and accepting that as final.

Gilbert in "The Critic as Artist," pt. 1, in *Intentions* (1891), repr. in Ellmann, 366-67.

Pater's essay "Leonardo da Vinci" in *Studies in the History of the Renaissance* (1873) contains the famous passage on the *La Gioconda* (also known as the *Mona Lisa*, to which Wilde alludes): "She is older than the rocks among which she sits; like the vampire, she has been dead many times. . . . "

If [Pater] be not among the greatest prose writers of our literature he is, at least, our greatest artist in prose; and though it may be admitted that the best style is that which seems an unconscious result rather than a conscious aim, still in these latter days when violent rhetoric does duty for eloquence and vulgarity usurps the name of nature, we should be grateful for a style that deliberately aims at perfection of form. . . .

"Mr. Pater's *Imaginary Portraits*," in *PMG* (June 11, 1887), repr. in *Reviews*, 175.

It is my golden book; I never travel anywhere without it; but it is the very flower of decadence: the last trumpet should have sounded the moment it was written.

Autobiography of W. B. Yeats (New York, 1965), repr. in Mikhail 1:145; slightly different versions appear in Robert Sherard's *The Life of Oscar Wilde* (New York, 1906), 311, and in Yeats's *Memoirs*, ed. Denis Donoghue (New York, 1973), 22.

Wilde alludes to Pater's *Studies in the History of the Renaissance* (1873).

PATHOLOGY

Pathology is rapidly becoming the basis of sensational literature, and in art, as in politics, there is a great future for monsters.

"Some Novels," in *Saturday Review* (May 7, 1887), repr. in *Reviews*, 166.

PEERAGE

You should study the Peerage, Gerald. It is the one book a young man about town should know thoroughly, and it is the best thing in fiction the English have ever done.

Lord Illingworth in *A Woman*, act 3.

A possible allusion to *Burke's Peerage, Baronetage, and Knightage* (1st ed., 1826) but more likely G. E. Cokayne's *Complete Peerage* (1884-98) .

PEOPLE

There are only two kinds of people who are really fascinating—people who know absolutely everything, and people who know absolutely nothing.

Lord Henry in *Dorian Gray*, ch. 7, the remark echoed by Lady Bracknell in *Earnest*, act 1.

It is absurd to divide people into good and bad. People are either charming or tedious.

Lord Darlington in *Fan*, act 1.

Good people, belonging as they do to the normal, and so, commonplace, type, are artistically uninteresting. Bad people are, from the point of view of art, fascinating studies. They represent colour, variety and strangeness. Good people exasperate one's reason; bad people stir one's imagination.

Letters, 259.

To the Editor, *St. James's Gazette* (June 26, 1890) on *Dorian Gray*.

PEOPLE, THE

Indeed, so little do ordinary people understand what thought really is, that they seem to imagine that, when they have said that a theory is dangerous, they have pronounced its condemnation, whereas it is only such theories that have any true intellectual value.

Gilbert in "The Critic as Artist," pt. 2, in *Intentions* (1891), repr. in Ellmann, 387-88.

As for the People, what of them and their authority? Perhaps of them and their authority one has spoken enough. Their authority is a thing blind, deaf, hideous, grotesque, tragic, amusing, serious and obscene. It is impossible for the artist to live with the People. All despots bribe. The people bribe and brutalize.

"The Soul of Man," repr. in Ellmann, 283.

The people and their rights bore me. I am sick of both. In these modern days, to be vulgar, illiterate, common and vicious, seems to give a man a marvellous infinity of rights that his honest fathers never dreamed of.

Prince Paul in *Vera*, act 2.

PERFECTION

JACK: You're quite perfect, Miss Fairfax.
GWENDOLEN: Oh! I hope I am not that. It would leave no room for developments, and I intend to develop in many directions.

Earnest, act 1.

What I mean by a perfect man is one who develops under perfect conditions; one who is not wounded, or worried, or maimed, or in danger. *Most personalities have been obliged to be rebels. Half their strength has been wasted in friction.*

"The Soul of Man," repr. in Ellmann, 262.

It is only by the continual contemplation of one's own perfection that one can hope to become perfect.

Quoted in: Small, 128.

PERSONALITY

It is true that, under existing conditions, a few men who have had private means of their own, such as Byron, Shelley, Browning, Victor Hugo, Baudelaire, and others, have been able to realise their personality more or less completely. Not one of these men ever did a single day's work for hire. They were relieved from poverty. They had an immense advantage. The question is whether it would be for the good of Individualism that such an advantage should be taken away.

"The Soul of Man," repr. in Ellmann, 260.

Personality is a very mysterious thing. A man cannot always be estimated by what he does. He may keep the law, and yet be worthless. He may break the law, and yet be fine. He may be bad, without ever doing anything bad. He may commit a sin against society, and yet realize through that sin his true perfection.

"The Soul of Man," repr. in Ellmann, 265.

The personality of the artist is not a thing the public should know anything about. It is too accidental.

Quoted in: "Mr. Oscar Wilde on Mr. Oscar Wilde," *St. James's Gazette* (January 18, 1895), unsigned but probably written by Robert Ross and Wilde; repr. in Mikhail 1:246.

*P*ESSIMISM

ALGERNON: I hope to-morrow will be a fine day, Lane.
LANE: It never is, sir.
ALGERNON: Lane, you're a perfect pessimist.
LANE: I do my best to give satisfaction, sir.

Earnest, act 1.

*P*HILANTHROPIST

Just as the philanthropist is the nuisance of the ethical sphere, so the nuisance of the intellectual sphere is the man who is so occupied in trying to educate others, that he has never had any time to educate himself.

Gilbert in "The Critic as Artist," pt. 2, in *Intentions* (1891), repr. in Ellmann, 387.

*P*ITY

I went into prison with a heart of stone, thinking only of my own pleasure, but now my heart is utterly broken—pity has entered into my heart. I have learned now that pity is the greatest and most beautiful thing in the world. And that is why I cannot bear ill-will towards those who caused my suffering and those who condemned me. . . .

Quoted in: Gide, ch. 3.

*P*LATITUDES

In modern life nothing produces such an effect as a good platitude. It makes the whole world kin.

Mrs. Cheveley in *Husband*, act 1, the second sentence derived from Shakespeare's *Troilus and Cressida*, act 3, sc. 3: "One touch of nature makes the whole world kin."

*P*LEASURE

Anything becomes a pleasure if one does it too often. That is one of the most important secrets of life. I should fancy, however, that murder is always a mistake. One should never do anything that one cannot talk about after dinner.

Lord Henry in *Dorian Gray*, ch. 19.

I adore simple pleasures. They are the last refuge of the complex.

Lord Henry in *Dorian Gray*, ch. 2; Lord Illingworth repeats these lines in *A Woman*, act 1.

Pleasure is Nature's test, her sign of approval. When we are happy, we are always good, but when we are good, we are not always happy.

Lord Henry in *Dorian Gray*, ch. 6.

Pleasure is what we take from others, Duty what we expect from others, and Genius what we deny to others.

Quoted in: Small, 127.

*P*OE, EDGAR ALLEN

Edgar Allen Poe insisted that no poem should take more than an hour to read, the essence of a work of art being its unity of impression and of effect. Still, it would be difficult to accept absolutely a canon of art which would place the *Divine Comedy* on the shelf. . . .

"A Modern Epic," in *PMG* (March 13, 1885), repr. in *Reviews*, 3-4.

$\mathcal{P}$OETRY

In Rossetti's poetry and the poetry of Morris, Swinburne and Tennyson a perfect precision and choice of language, a style flawless and fearless, a seeking for all sweet and precious melodies and a sustaining consciousness of the musical value of each word are opposed to that value which is merely intellectual.

"English Renaissance," pub. in *Miscellanies*, 253.

It is not an increased moral sense, an increased moral supervision that your literature needs. Indeed, one should never talk of a moral or an immoral poem—poems are either well written or badly written, that is all.

"English Renaissance," pub. in *Miscellanies*, 267; the second sentence closely echoes *Dorian Gray*, Preface.

A basic principle of Aestheticism.

Poetry should be like a crystal, it should make life more beautiful and less real.

Letters, 217.

Written to the artist and writer W. Graham Robertson in early 1888.

It would be sad indeed if the many volumes of poems that are every year published in London found no readers but the authors themselves and the authors' relations; and the real philanthropist should recognize it as part of his duties to buy every new book of verse that appears. Sometimes, we acknowledge, he will be disappointed, often he will be bored; still now and then he will be amply rewarded for his reckless benevolence.

"News from Parnassus," in *PMG* (April 12, 1886), repr. in *Reviews*, 51.

That incommunicable element of artistic delight . . . comes from what Keats called the "sensuous life of verse," the element of song in the singing, made so pleasurable to us by that wonder of motion which often has its origin in mere musical impulse, and in painting is to be sought for, from the subject never, but from the pictorial charm only—the scheme and symphony of the colour, the satisfying beauty of the design. . . .

"L'Envoi," in Rennell Rodd's *Rose Leaf and Apple Leaf* (Philadelphia, 1882), repr. in *Miscellanies*, 30.

The poetry and music of Ireland have been not merely the luxury of the rich, but the very bulwark of patriotism, the very seed and flower of liberty.

Quoted in: Robert D. Pepper, ed., *Irish Poets and Poetry of the Nineteenth Century* (San Francisco, 1972), 28.

A report of Wilde's lecture in the *San Francisco Chronicle* (April 6, 1882).

*P*OETS

The domain of the painter is, as I suggested before, widely different from that of the poet. To the latter belongs life in its full and absolute entirety; not merely the beauty that men look at, but the beauty that men listen to also, not merely the momentary grace of form or the transient gladness of colour, but the whole sphere of feeling, the perfect cycle of thought.

Gilbert in "The Critic as Artist," pt. 1, in *Intentions* (1891), repr. in Ellmann, 369.

I suppose that the poet will sing or the artist will paint regardless whether the world praises or blames; he has his own world and is independent of his fellow men, but the ordinary handicraftsman is almost dependent upon your pleasure and opinion and upon the influences which surround him for his knowledge of form and colour.

"The Decorative Arts," in O'Brien, 152.

And so it comes that he who seems to stand most remote from his age is he who mirrors it best, because he has stripped life of what is accidental and transitory....

"English Renaissance," pub. in *Miscellanies*, 258.

To the poet all times and places are one; the stuff he deals with is eternal and eternally the same: no theme is inept, no past or present preferable. The steam whistle will not affright him nor the flutes of Arcadia weary him: for him there is but one time, the artistic moment; but one law, the law of form; but one land, the land of Beauty—a land removed indeed from the real world and yet more sensuous because more enduring....

"English Renaissance," pub. in *Miscellanies*, 258.

I am afraid you are going to be a poet: how tragic! How terribly tragic! In the waters of Helicon there is death—the only death worth dying.

Letters, 812.

Written to a young student Louis Wilkinson in November 1899 from France; the waters of Helicon, the largest mountain of Boeotia in Greece, were a source of inspiration, hence associated with the Muses.

The poet's noblest verse, the dramatist's greatest scene, deal always with death; because the highest function of the artist is to make perceived the beauty of failure.

Quoted in: Housman, 29.

Poets, you know, are always ahead of science; all the great discoveries of science have been stated before in poetry. So far as science comes in contact with our school, we love its practical side; but we think it absurd to seek to make the material include the spiritual, to make the body mean the soul, to say that one emotion is only a secretion of sugar, and another nothing but a contraction of the spine.

Quoted in: Lewis and Smith, 65.

An interview reported in the *Philadelphia Press* (January 17, 1882).

POLITICS

Alien then from any wild, political passions, or from the harsh voice of a rude people in revolt, as our English Renaissance must seem, in its passionate cult of pure beauty, its flawless devotion, its exclusive and sensitive nature, it is to the French Revolution that we must look for the most primary factor of its production, the first condition of its birth. . . .

"English Renaissance," pub. in *Miscellanies*, 245.

LADY BASILDON: I don't know how the unfortunate men in the House [of Commons] stand these long debates.
LORD GORING: By never listening.
LADY BASILDON: Really?
LORD GORING: Of course. You see, it is a very dangerous thing to listen. If one listens one may be convinced; and a man who allows himself to be convinced by an argument is a thoroughly unreasonable person.

Husband, act 1.

POPULARITY

Popularity is the crown of laurel which the world puts on bad art. Whatever is popular is wrong.

"Lecture to Art Students," of the Royal Academy (June 30, 1883), pub. in *Miscellanies*, 312.

$\mathcal{P}$ORTRAITS

Every portrait that is painted with feeling is a portrait of the artist, not of
the sitter.

Basil Hallward in *Dorian Gray*, ch. 1.

The picture, changed or unchanged, would be to him the visible emblem of
conscience. He would resist temptation. He would not see Lord Henry any
more—would not, at any rate, listen to those subtle poisonous theories
that in Basil Hallward's garden had first stirred within him the passion for
impossible things.

Dorian Gray, ch. 7.

This portrait would be to him the most magical of mirrors. As it had
revealed to him his own body, so it would reveal to him his own soul. . . .
When the blood crept from its face, and left behind a pallid mask of chalk
with leaden eyes, he would keep the glamour of boyhood. . . . Like the
gods of the Greeks, he would be strong, and fleet, and joyous. What did it
matter what happened to the coloured image on the canvas? He would be
safe.

Dorian Gray, ch. 8.

$\mathcal{P}$RAYER

Prayer must never be answered: if it is, it ceases to be prayer, and becomes a
correspondence.

Quoted in: Housman, 43.

$\mathcal{P}$RE-RAPHAELITES

If you inquire about the pre-Raphaelites you will hear something about an
eccentric lot of young men to whom a sort of divine crookedness and holy

awkwardness in drawing were the chief objects of art. To know nothing about their great men is one of the necessary elements of English education.

"English Renaissance," pub. in *Miscellanies*, 249-50.

In England, then as now, it was enough for a man to try and produce any serious beautiful work to lose all his rights as a citizen; and besides this, the Pre-Raphaelite Brotherhood—among whom the names of Dante Rossetti, Holman Hunt and Millais will be familiar to you—had on their side three things that the English public never forgives: youth, power and enthusiasm.

"English Renaissance," pub. in *Miscellanies*, 250.

*P*REACHING

I won't tell you that I don't want to preach to you. I remember Harry saying once that every man who turned himself into an amateur curate for the moment always began by saying that, and then proceeded to break his word. I do want to preach to you. I want you to lead such a life as will make the world respect you.

Basil Hallward to Dorian in *Dorian Gray*, ch. 12.
Basil had heard rumors of Dorian's disreputable behavior.

My dear boy, you are really beginning to moralize. You will soon be going about like the converted, and the revivalist, warning people against all the sins of which you have grown tired.

Lord Henry in *Dorian Gray*, ch. 19.
Reacting to Dorian's urging that Lord Henry never lend the "poisonous" book that had corrupted him to anyone else.

*P*RETENSION

If you pretend to be good, the world takes you very seriously. If you pretend to be bad, it doesn't. Such is the astounding stupidity of optimism.

Lord Darlington in *Fan*, act 1.

In old days nobody pretended to be a bit better than his neighbours. In fact, to be a bit better than one's neighbour was considered excessively vulgar and middle-class. Nowadays, with our modern mania for morality, everyone has to pose as a paragon of purity, incorruptibility, and all the other seven deadly virtues—and what is the result . . . ? Not a year passes in England without somebody disappearing.

Mrs. Cheveley in *Husband*, act 1.

Price

Nowadays people know the price of everything and the value of nothing.

Lord Henry in *Dorian Gray*, ch. 4, in slightly different form as Lord Darlington's response to the question "What is a cynic?" in *Fan*, act 3: "A man who knows. . . . "

Principles

I like persons better than principles, and I like persons with no principles better than anything else in the world.

Lord Henry in *Dorian Gray*, ch. 1.

Lord Henry had not yet come in. He was always late on principle, his principle being that punctuality is the thief of time.

Dorian Gray, ch. 4.

There is nothing to be said in favour of anyone's principles. There is much to be said in favour of everyone's prejudices.

Quoted in: Small, 128.

Prison and Prisoners

Mankind has been continually entering the prisons of Puritanism, Philistinism, Sensualism, Fanaticism, and turning the key on its own spirit:

but after a time there is a an enormous desire for higher freedom—for self-preservation.

"Commonplace Book," pub. in Smith and Helfand, 110.

Prison-life makes one see people and things as they really are. That is why it turns one to stone. It is the people outside who are deceived by the illusion of a life in constant motion.

Letters, 514.
Written to Robert Ross on Apr. 1, 1897 from Reading Prison, partly pub. as *De Profundis* (1905).

[I] wish we could meet to talk over the many prisons of life—prisons of stone, prisons of passion, prisons of intellect, prisons of morality, and the rest. All limitations, external or internal, are prison-walls, and life is a limitation.

More Letters, 165.
Written in February 1898 from France to the author and Socialist R. B. Cunninghame Graham, once imprisoned himself.

Each narrow cell in which we dwell
Is a foul and dark latrine,
And the fetid breath of living Death
Chokes up each grated screen,
And all, but Lust is turned to dust
In Humanity's machine.

Reading Gaol, lines 571-76, repr. in *Poems* (1997).

This too I know—and wise it were
If each could know the same—
That every prison that men build
Is built with bricks of shame,
And bound with bars lest Christ should see
How men their brothers maim.

Reading Gaol, lines 547-52, repr. in *Poems* (1997).

𝒫ROFESSIONS

Each of the professions means a prejudice. The necessity for a career forces every one to take sides.

Gilbert in "The Critic as Artist," pt. 2, in *Intentions* (1891), repr. in Ellmann, 385.

PROPERTY

Property not merely has duties, but has so many duties that its possession to any large extent is a bore. It involves endless claims upon one, endless attention to business, endless bother. If property had simply pleasures, we could stand it; but its duties make it unbearable. In the interest of the rich we must get rid of it.

"The Soul of Man," repr. in Ellmann, 258.

In *Earnest*, act 1, Lady Bracknell remarks: "What between the duties expected of one during one's lifetime, and the duties exacted from one after one's death, land has ceased to be either a profit or a pleasure."

The recognition of private property has really harmed Individualism, and obscured it, by confusing a man with what he possesses. It has led Individualism entirely astray. It has made gain not growth its aim. So that man thought that the important thing was to have, and did not know that the important thing is to be. *The true perfection of man lies, not in what man has, but in what man is.*

"The Soul of Man," repr. in Ellmann, 261.

The last two sentences echo Emerson's essay "Self-Reliance" in *Essays*, First Series (1841).

PROSE

I hold that, in prose at any rate, correctness should always be subordinate to artistic effect and musical cadence. . . .

Letters, 258.

Written to the Editor, *St. James's Gazette*, June 26, 1890, in defense of *Dorian Gray*.

Writers of poetical prose are rarely good poets. They may crowd their lines with gorgeous epithet and resplendent phrase . . . but if their work lacks the true rhythmical life of verse, if their method is devoid of the self-restraint of the real artist, all their efforts are of very little avail. . . . Indeed poetry may be said to require far more self-restraint than prose. . . . It is, in one sense, the most self-conscious of all the arts, as it is never a means to an end, but always an end in itself.

"Sir Edwin Arnold's Last Volume," in *PMG* (December 11, 1888), repr. in *Reviews*, 365.

A review of *With Sa'di in the Garden; or, The Book of Love*.

PROSTITUTION

... one pale woman all alone,
The daylight kissing her wan hair,
Loitered beneath the gas lamps' flare,
With lips of flame and heart of stone.

> "Impression du Matin," in *World* (March 2, 1881), repr. in *Poems* (1997).

PRUDENCE

Thin-lipped wisdom spoke at her from the worn chair, hinted at prudence, quoted from that book of cowardice whose author apes the name of common sense. She did not listen. She was free in her prison of passion. Her prince, Prince Charming, was with her.

> *Dorian Gray*, ch. 5.
>
> Mrs. Vane is reported as speaking to her daughter Sibyl, in love with Dorian, "Prince Charming."

PSYCHOLOGY

[Dorian] used to wonder at the shallow psychology of those who conceive the ego in man as a thing simple, permanent, reliable, and of one essence. To him, man was a being with myriad lives and myriad sensations, a complex multiform creature that bore within itself strange legacies of thought and passion, and whose very flesh was tainted with the monstrous maladies of the dead.

> *Dorian Gray*, ch. 11.

PUBLIC, THE

The more the public is interested in artists, the less it is interested in art.

> Quoted in: "Mr. Oscar Wilde on Mr. Oscar Wilde," *St. James's Gazette* (January 18, 1895), unsigned but probably written by Robert Ross and Wilde; repr. in Mikhail 1:246.

℘UNISHMENT

In all things connected with money I have had a luck so extraordinary that sometimes it has made me almost afraid. I remember having read somewhere, in some strange book, that when the gods wish to punish us they answer our prayers.

Sir Robert Chiltern in *Husband*, act 2.

℘UPPETS

There are many advantages in puppets. They never argue. They have no crude views about art. They have no private lives. We are never bothered by accounts of their virtues, or bored by recitals of their vices; and when they are out of an engagement they never do good in public or save people from drowning. . . .

Letters, 311.
Written to the Editor, *Daily Telegraph*, on February 19, 1892.

℘URITANISM

Puritanism is never so offensive and destructive as when it deals with art matters. It is there that its influence is radically wrong.

Letters, 261.
Written to the Editor, *St. James's Gazette*, on June 27, 1890 in defense of *Dorian Gray*.

℘URITY

Men who talked grossly became silent when Dorian Gray entered the room. There was something in the purity of his face that rebuked them. His mere presence seemed to recall to them the memory of the innocence that they had tarnished. They wondered how one so charming and graceful as he was could have escaped the stain of an age that was at once sordid and sensual.

Dorian Gray, ch. 11.

READING

We live in an age that reads too much to be wise, and that thinks too much to be beautiful.

Lord Henry in *Dorian Gray*, ch. 8.

Oh! it is absurd to have a hard-and-fast rule about what one should read and what one shouldn't. More than half of modern culture depends on what one shouldn't read.

Algernon Moncrieff in *Earnest*, act 1.

Coming along I begged to be allowed to read [*The Daily Chronicle*] in the train. "No!" Then I suggested I might be allowed to read it upside down. This they consented to allow, and I read all the way *The Daily Chronicle* upside down, and never enjoyed it so much. It's really the only way to read newspapers.

Quoted in: "Reminiscences" by Ada Leverson, repr. in Wyndham, 121.

On being transferred from one prison to another.

REALISM

There are moments when we feel that but little artistic pleasure is to be gained from the study of the modern realistic school. Its works are powerful, but they are painful, and after a time we tire of their harshness, their violence and their crudity. They exaggerate the importance of facts and underrate the importance of fiction.

"A Good Historical Novel," in *PMG* (August 8, 1887), repr. in *Reviews*, 176.

A review of Stephen Coleridge's *Demetrius*.

REBIRTH

I call it our English Renaissance because it is indeed a sort of new birth of the spirit of man, like the great Italian Renaissance of the fifteenth century, in its desire for a more gracious and comely way of life, its passion for physical beauty, its exclusive attention to form, its seeking for new subjects for poetry, new forms of art, new intellectual and imaginative enjoyments. . . .

"English Renaissance," pub. in *Miscellanies*, 243.

RECOGNITION

WILDE: . . . you recently published a book called *The Religion of a Literary Man*. . . . Well, you were very unkind to me in that book . . . most unkind!

LE GALLIENNE: . . . Why, Oscar, I don't know what you mean. . . . Why, I can't remember that I even mentioned your name in it.

WILDE: Ah! Richard, that was just it.

Quoted in: Richard Le Gallienne's *The Romantic '90s* (1926), ch. 5; repr. in Mikhail, 2:396.

REFLECTIONS

One should not look at anything. Neither at things, nor at people should one look. Only in mirrors is it well to look, for mirrors do but show us masks.

Herod in *Salome* (1894).

REJECTION

Get hence, you loathsome Mystery! Hideous animal, get hence! You wake in me each bestial sense, you make me what I would not be. You make my creed a barren sham, you wake foul dreams of sensual life. . . .

The Sphinx, lines 167-69 (1894), repr. in *Poems* (1997).

RELATIONS

After a good dinner one can forgive anybody, even one's own relations.

Lady Caroline in *A Woman*, act 2.

On her brother, the "Infamous" Lord Henry Weston.

I love hearing my relations abused. It is the only thing that makes me put up with them at all. Relations are simply a tedious pack of people, who haven't got the remotest knowledge of how to live, nor the smallest instinct about when to die.

> Algernon Moncrieff in *Earnest*, act 1.

RELIGION

As for the Church I cannot conceive anything better for the culture of a country than the presence in it of a body of men whose duty it is to believe in the supernatural, to perform daily miracles, and to keep alive that mythopoeic faculty which is so essential for the imagination.

> Vivian in "The Decay of Lying," in *Intentions* (1891), repr. in Ellmann, 317.

Religion springs from religious feeling, art from artistic feeling: you never get one from the other; unless you have the right root you will not get the right flower; and, if a man sees in a cloud the chariot of an angel, he will probably paint it very unlike a cloud.

> "Lecture to Art Students," of the Royal Academy (June 30, 1883), pub. in *Miscellanies*, 318.

Religions die when they are proved to be true. Science is the record of dead religions.

> "Phrases and Philosophies," repr. in Ellmann, 433.

RENAISSANCE

As far as the Renaissance is concerned what humanity demanded at that splendid crisis, when the world-spirit was in the throes of travail of things evil and good—was not new theories of conduct or even its practice—not order—not virtue even—but free scope for the intellect—the throwing off of authority to breathe again in the free frank air where nothing stood between men's eyes and the sun of truth. . . .

> "Commonplace Book," pub. in Smith and Helfand, 124.

REPUTATION

[My mother] and my father had bequeathed me a name they had made noble and honoured not merely in Literature, Art, Archaeology and Science, but in the public history of my own country in its evolution as a nation. I had disgraced that name eternally. I had made it a low byword among low people.

Letters, 458.
Written to Alfred Douglas in early 1897 from Reading Prison, partly pub. as De Profundis (1905).

RESOLVE

It is always with the best intentions that the worst work is done.

Gilbert in "The Critic as Artist," pt. 2, in Intentions (1891), repr. in Ellmann, 400.

REVISING

WILDE: I was working on the proof one of my poems all the morning and took out a comma.
SHERARD: And in the afternoon?
WILDE: In the afternoon—well, I put it back again.

Quoted in: Robert Sherard, Oscar Wilde: The Story of an Unhappy Friendship (1905; repr. New York, 1970), 72.

RHYME

Rhyme, that exquisite echo which in the Muse's hollow hill creates and answers its own voice; rhyme, which in the hands of the real artist becomes not merely a material element of metrical beauty, but a spiritual element of thought and passion also . . . or opening by mere sweetness and suggestion of sound some golden door at which the Imagination itself had knocked in vain . . . became in Robert Browning's hands a grotesque misshapen thing, which at times made him masquerade in poetry as a low comedian. . . .

Gilbert in "The Critic as Artist," pt. 1, in *Intentions* (1891), repr. in Ellmann, 345.

RITUALS: RELIGIOUS

He loved to kneel down on the cold marble pavement, and watch the priest, in his stiff flowered dalmatic, slowly and with white hands moving aside the veil of the tabernacle, or raising aloft the jewelled lantern-shaped monstrance with that pallid wafer that at times . . . is indeed the "*panis caelestis,*" the bread of angels, or, robed in the garments of the Passion of Christ, breaking the Host into the chalice, and smiting his breast for his sins.

Dorian Gray, ch. 11.

Dorian, reluctant to convert to Roman Catholicism, nevertheless admires the beauty of church ritual.

ROMANCE

Romance lives by repetition, and repetition converts an appetite into an art. Besides, each time that one loves is the only time one has ever loved. . . . We can have in life but one great experience at best, and the secret of life is to reproduce that experience as often as possible.

Lord Henry in *Dorian Gray*, ch. 17.

What you have told me is quite a romance, a romance of art one might call it, and the worst of having a romance of any kind is that it leaves one so unromantic.

Lord Henry in *Dorian Gray*, ch. 1.

Commenting on Basil Hallward's emotional reaction to Dorian.

I really don't see anything romantic in proposing. It is very romantic to be in love. But there is nothing romantic about a definite proposal. Why, one may be accepted. One usually is, I believe. Then the excitement is all over.

Algernon Moncrieff in *Earnest*, act 1.

Twenty years of romance make a woman look like a ruin; but twenty years of marriage make her something like a public building.

Lord Illingworth in *A Woman*, act 1.

*R*OMANTICISM

Unconsciously he defines for me the lines of a fresh school, a school that is to have in it all the passion of the romantic spirit, all the perfection of the spirit that is Greek. The harmony of soul and body—how much that is! We in our madness have separated the two, and have invented a realism that is vulgar, an ideality that is void.

Basil Hallward in *Dorian Gray*, ch. 1.
Commenting on Dorian.

He must have a truly romantic nature, for he weeps when there is nothing at all to weep about.

The Catherine Wheel in "The Remarkable Rocket," in *The Happy Prince*.
Concerning the Rocket.

Romantic poetry, too, is essentially the poetry of impressions, being like that latest school of painting, the school of Whistler and Albert Moore, in its choice of situation as opposed to subject; in its dealing with the exceptions rather than with the types of life; in its brief intensity; in what one might call its fiery-coloured momentariness. . . .

"L'Envoi," in Rennell Rodd's *Rose Leaf and Apple Leaf* (Philadelphia, 1882), repr. in *Miscellanies*, 38.

*R*OSSETTI, *CHRISTINA*

Much as I admire Miss Rossetti's work, her subtle choice of words, her rich imagery, her artistic *naïveté*, wherein curious notes of strangeness and simplicity are fantastically blended together, I cannot but think that Mr. Swinburne has, with noble and natural loyalty, placed her on too lofty a pedestal.

"English Poetesses," in *The Queen* (December 8, 1888), repr. in Ellmann, 101.

RUIN

I ruined myself: and . . . nobody, great or small, can be ruined except by his own hand.

Letters, 465.

Written to Alfred Douglas in early 1897 from Reading Prison, partly pub. as *De Profundis* (1905).

My ruin came, not from too great individualism of life, but from too little.

Letters, 491.

Written to Alfred Douglas in early 1897 from Reading Prison, partly pub. as *De Profundis* (1905).

Why is it that one runs to one's ruin? Why has destruction such a fascination? Why, when one stands on a pinnacle, must one throw oneself down? No one knows, but things are so.

Letters, 629.

Written to his friend Carlos Blacker in August 1897 from France.

RUNNING AWAY

It is said, of course, that [Mrs Allonby] ran away twice before she was married. But you know how unfair people often are. I myself don't believe she ran away more than once.

Lady Caroline in *A Woman*, act 1.

RUSKIN, JOHN

Who cares whether Mr. Ruskin's views on Turner are sound or not? What does it matter? That mighty and majestic prose of his, so fervid and so fiery-coloured in its noble eloquence, so rich in its elaborate symphonic music, so sure and certain, at its best, in subtle choice of word and epithet, is at least as great a work of art as any of those

wonderful sunsets that bleach or rot on their corrupted canvases in
England's Gallery. . . .

Gilbert in "The Critic as Artist," pt. 1, in *Intentions* (1891), repr. in Ellmann, 366.

In his *Modern Painters* (1843-60), Ruskin defended J. M. W. Turner's controversial paintings.

There is in you something of prophet, of priest, and of poet, and to you the
gods gave eloquence such as they have given to none other, so that your
message might come to us with the fire of passion, and the marvel of
music, making the deaf to hear, and the blind to see.

Letters, 218.

Written to a critic May 1888.

Master indeed of the knowledge of all noble living and of the wisdom of all
spiritual things will [Ruskin] be to us ever, seeing that it was he who by the
magic of his presence and the music of his lips taught us at Oxford that
enthusiasm for beauty which is the secret of Hellenism, and that desire for
creation which is the secret of life . . . and yet in his art criticism, his
estimate of the joyous element of art, his whole method of approaching
art, we are no longer with him; for the keystone to his aesthetic system is
ethical always.

"L'Envoi," in Rennell Rodd's *Rose Leaf and Apple Leaf* (Philadelphia, 1882), repr. in *Miscellanies*, 31-32.

*S*ACREDNESS

LORD HENRY: . . . what are your actual relations with Sibyl Vane?
DORIAN: Harry! Sibyl Vane is sacred!
LORD HENRY: It is only the sacred things that are worth touching. . . .

Dorian Gray, ch. 4.

*S*ACRILEGE

A feeling of pain crept over him as he thought of the desecration that was
in store for the fair face on the canvas. Once, in boyish mockery of

Narcissus, he had kissed, or feigned to kiss, those painted lips that now
smiled so cruelly at him.

> Dorian Gray, ch. 8.
>
> On Dorian's narcissism.

SAINTS

The only difference between the saint and the sinner is that every saint has
a past, and every sinner has a future.

> Lord Illingworth in A Woman, act 3.

SALOMÉ

Personally, to have my première [of Salomé] in Paris instead of in London is
a great honour, and one that I appreciate sincerely. The pleasure and pride
that I have experienced in the whole affair has been that Madame Sarah
Bernhardt, who is undoubtedly the greatest artist on any stage, should have
been charmed and fascinated by my play and should have wished to act it.

> Quoted in: "The Censure and Salomé," Pall Mall Budget (June 30, 1892), repr. in Mikhail 1:186.
>
> An interview after hearing that Salomé had been refused a license for the stage.

SAND, GEORGE

Perhaps [George Sand] valued good intentions in art a little too much, and
she hardly understood that art for art's sake is not meant to express the
final cause of art but is merely a formula of creation; but, as she herself had
scaled Parnassus, we must not quarrel at her bringing Proletarianism with
her. For George Sand must be ranked among our poetic geniuses.

> "The Letters of a Great Woman," in PMG (March 6, 1886), repr. in Reviews, 49.

Of all the artists of this century [George Sand] was the most altruistic; she
felt every one's misfortunes except her own.

> "The Letters of a Great Woman," in PMG (March 6, 1886), repr. in Reviews, 48.

Scandals

I love scandals about other people, but scandals about myself don't interest me. They have not got the charm of novelty.

Dorian in *Dorian Gray*, ch. 12.

LORD WINDERMERE: What is the difference between scandal and gossip?
CECIL GRAHAM: Oh! gossip is charming! History is merely gossip. But scandal is gossip made tedious by morality.

Fan, act 3.

Suppose that when I leave this house I drive down to some newspaper office, and give them this scandal and the proofs of it! Think of their loathsome joy, of the delight they would have in dragging you down, of the mud and mire they would plunge you in. Think of the hypocrite with his greasy smile penning his leading article, and arranging the foulness of the public placard.

Mrs. Cheveley to Sir Robert Chiltern in *Husband*, act 1.

An eerie passage anticipating the reaction of the press when Wilde was arrested in 1895.

Scholarship

Dr. Chasuble is a most learned man. He has never written a single book, so you can imagine how much he knows.

Cecily Cardew in *Earnest*, act 2.

Schools

I remember bright young faces, and grey misty quadrangles, Greek forms passing through Gothic cloisters, life playing among ruins, and, what I love best in the world, Poetry and Paradox dancing together!

Letters, 181.

A remembrance of Oxford: written to H. C. Marillier, an acquaintance, in November 1885.

Schopenhauer, Arthur

Schopenhauer has analysed the pessimism that characterises modern thought, but Hamlet invented it. The world has become sad because a puppet was once melancholy.

Vivian in "The Decay of Lying," in *Intentions* (1891), repr. in Ellmann, 308.

Science

When we have fully discovered the scientific laws that govern life, we shall realize that the one person who has more illusions than the dreamer is the man of action. He, indeed, knows neither the origin of his deeds nor their results.

Gilbert in "The Critic as Artist," pt. 1, in *Intentions* (1891), repr. in Ellmann, 359.

Science is out of the reach of morals, for her eyes are fixed upon eternal truths. Art is out of the reach of morals, for her eyes are fixed upon things beautiful and immortal and ever-changing. To morals belong the lower and less intellectual spheres.

Gilbert in "The Critic as Artist," pt. 2, in *Intentions* (1891), repr. in Ellmann, 394.

SIR ROBERT CHILTERN: You think science cannot grapple with the problem of women?
MRS. CHEVELEY: Science can never grapple with the irrational. That is why it has no future before it, in this world.
SIR ROBERT: And women represent the irrational.
MRS. CHEVELEY: Well-dressed women do.

Husband, act 1.

Secrets

CECILY: I keep a diary in order to enter the wonderful secrets of my life. If I didn't write them down I should probably forget all about them.
MISS PRISM: Memory, my dear Cecily, is the diary that we all carry about with us.

CECILY: Yes, but it usually chronicles the things that have never happened, and couldn't possibly have happened. I believe that Memory is responsible for nearly all the the three-volume novels that Mudie sends us.

Earnest, act 2.

Mudie's was a popular circulating library at the time.

I have grown to love secrecy. It seems to be the one thing that can make modern life mysterious or marvellous to us. The commonest thing is delightful if one only hides it.

Basil Hallward in *Dorian Gray*, ch. 1.

No man should have a secret from his own wife. She invariably finds it out. Women have a wonderful instinct about things. They can discover every-thing except the obvious.

Lord Goring in *Husband*, act 2.

There is not a single wretched man in this wretched place along with me who does not stand in symbolic relations to the very secret of life. For the secret of life is suffering. It is what is hidden behind everything.

Letters, 473.

Written to Alfred Douglas in early 1897 from Reading Prison, partly pub. as *De Profundis* (1905).

MRS. ALLONBY: The secret of life is never to have an emotion that is unbecoming.

LADY STUTFIELD: The secret of life is to appreciate the pleasure of being terribly, terribly deceived.

KELVIL: The secret of life is to resist temptation, Lady Stutfield.

A Woman, act 3.

There is no secret of life. Life's aim, if it has one, is simply to be always looking for temptations. There are not nearly enough. I sometimes pass a whole day without coming across a single one. It is quite dreadful. It makes one so nervous about the future.

Lord Illingworth in *A Woman*, act 3.

SELF, THE

Now, nothing should be able to harm a man except himself. Nothing should be able to rob a man at all. What a man really has, is what is in him. What is outside of him should be a matter of no importance.

"The Soul of Man," repr. in Ellmann, 262.

The first sentence echoes Emerson's essay "Compensation" in *Essays*, First Series (1841).

SELFISHNESS

BASIL HALLWARD: . . . surely, if one lives merely for one's self, Harry, one pays a terrible price for doing so?

LORD HENRY: Yes, we are overcharged for everything nowadays.

Dorian Gray, ch. 6.

It takes a thoroughly selfish age, like our own, to deify self-sacrifice.

Gilbert in "The Critic as Artist," pt. 2, in *Intentions* (1891), repr. in Ellmann, 386.

Selfishness is not living as one wishes to live, it is asking others to live as one wishes to live.

"The Soul of Man," repr. in Ellmann, 285.

SENSES

It appeared to Dorian Gray that the true nature of the senses had never been understood, and that they had remained savage and animal merely because the world had sought to starve them into submission or to kill them by pain, instead of aiming at making them elements of a new spirituality, of which a fine instinct for beauty was to be the dominant characteristic.

Dorian Gray, ch. 11.

The worship of the senses has often, with much justice, been decried, men feeling a natural instinct of terror about passions and sensations that seem stronger than themselves, and that they are conscious of sharing with the less highly organized forms of existence.

Dorian Gray, ch. 11.

SENTIMENTALITY

They miss their aim, too, these philanthropists and sentimentalists of our day, who are always chattering to one about one's duty to one's neighbour. For the development of the race depends on the development of the individual, and where self-culture has ceased to be the ideal, the intellectual standard is instantly lowered, and, often, ultimately lost.

Gilbert in "The Critic as Artist," pt. 2, in *Intentions* (1891), repr. in Ellmann, 386.

A sentimentalist, my dear Darlington, is a man who sees an absurd value in everything, and doesn't know the market price of any single thing.

Cecil Graham in *Fan*, act 3.

One must have a heart of stone to read the death of Little Nell without laughing.

Quoted in: "Reminiscences" by Ada Leverson, repr. in Wyndham, 119.

Alluding to the death of Dickens's angelic child in *The Old Curiosity Shop* (1841).

SEPARATION

A man whose desire is to be something separate from himself, to be a Member of Parliament, or a successful grocer, or a prominent solicitor, or a judge, or something equally tedious, invariably succeeds in being what he wants to be. That is his punishment. Those who want a mask have to wear it.

Letters, 487-88.

Written to Alfred Douglas in early 1897 from Reading Prison, partly pub. as *De Profundis* (1905).

SEX

The first these ten years, and it will be the last. It was like cold mutton. But tell it in England, for it will entirely restore my character.

Quoted in: "The Tragic Generation," pt. 14, in *The Autobiography of W. B. Yeats* (New York, 1965).

On having visited a brothel in Dieppe at the urging of the poet Ernest Dowson, who had "pressed upon him the necessity of acquiring 'a more wholesome taste.' "

SHAKESPEARE

Action being limited would have left Shakespeare unsatisfied and unexpressed; and, just as it is because he did nothing that he has been able to achieve everything, so it is because he never speaks to us of himself in his plays that his plays reveal him to us absolutely, and show us his true nature and temperament far more completely than do those strange and exquisite sonnets, even, in which he bares to crystal eyes the secret closet of his heart.

Gilbert in "The Critic as Artist," pt. 2, in *Intentions* (1891), repr. in Ellmann, 389.

[Critics] will call upon Shakespeare—they always do—and will quote that hackneyed passage about Art holding the mirror up to Nature, forgetting that this unfortunate aphorism is deliberately said by Hamlet in order to convince the bystanders of his absolute insanity in all art-matters.

Vivian in "The Decay of Lying," in *Intentions* (1891), repr. in Ellmann, 306.

Hamlet delivers the aphorism in his speech to the actors (act 3, scene 2).

The passages in Shakespeare—and they are many—where the language is uncouth, vulgar, exaggerated, fantastic, obscene even, are entirely due to Life calling for an echo of her own voice, and rejecting the intervention of beautiful style, through which alone should Life be suffered to find expression.

Vivian in "The Decay of Lying," in *Intentions* (1891), repr. in Ellmann, 302.

I have been right, Basil, haven't I, to take my love out of poetry, and to find my wife in Shakespeare's plays? Lips that Shakespeare taught to speak have whispered their secret in my ear. I have had the arms of Rosalind around me, and kissed Juliet on the mouth.

Dorian to Basil Hallward in *Dorian Gray*, ch. 6.

Allusions to the actress Sibyl Vane, who performed in Shakespeare's plays.

Of course the aesthetic value of Shakespeare's plays does not, in the slightest degree, depend on their facts, but on the Truth, and Truth is independent of facts always, inventing or selecting them at pleasure. But still Shakespeare's use of facts is a most interesting part of his method of work, and shows us his attitude towards the stage, and his relations to the great art of illusion.

"The Truth of Masks," in *Intentions* (1891), repr. in Ellmann, 423.

*S*HALLOWNESS

It is only shallow people who do not judge by appearances.

Lord Henry in *Dorian Gray*, ch. 2, the epigram repeated in a letter to W. E. Combe in December 1892 (*Letters*, 324).

It is only shallow people who require years to get rid of an emotion. A man who is master of himself can end a sorrow as easily as he can invent a pleasure. I don't want to be at the mercy of my emotions. I want to use them, to enjoy them, and to dominate them.

Dorian in *Dorian Gray*, ch. 9.

The creed of the dandy.

The supreme vice is shallowness.

Letters, 425.

Written from Reading Prison to Alfred Douglas, early 1897, partly published as *De Profundis* (1905).

Only the shallow know themselves.

"Phrases and Philosophies," repr. in Ellmann, 434.

*S*HELLEY, PERCY BYSSHE

Like Byron, [Shelley] got out of England as soon as possible. But he was not so well known. If the English had had any idea of what a great poet he really was, they would have fallen on him with tooth and nail, and made his life as unbearable to him as they possibly could.

"The Soul of Man," repr. in Ellmann, 262.

SIMILARITY

It is a humiliating confession, but we are all of us made out of the same stuff. In Falstaff there is something of Hamlet, in Hamlet there is not a little of Falstaff. The fat knight has his moods of melancholy, and the young prince his moments of coarse humour. Where we differ from each other is purely in accidentals: in dress, manner, tone of voice, religious opinions, personal appearance, tricks of habit. . . .

> Vivian in "The Decay of Lying," in *Intentions* (1891), repr. in Ellmann, 297.

SIN

By its curiosity, Sin increases the experience of the race. Through its intensified assertion of individualism, it saves us from monotony of type. In its rejection of the current notions about morality, it is one with the higher ethics.

> Gilbert in "The Critic as Artist," pt. 1, in *Intentions* (1891), repr. in Ellmann, 360.

What is termed Sin is an essential element of progress. Without it the world would stagnate, or grow old, or become colourless.

> Gilbert in "The Critic as Artist," pt. 1, in *Intentions* (1891), repr. in Ellmann, 360.

All sins, as theologians weary not of reminding us, are sins of disobedience. When that high spirit, that morning-star of evil, fell from heaven, it was as a rebel that he fell.

> *Dorian Gray*, ch. 16.

One pays for one's sins, and then one pays again, and all one's life one pays.

> Mrs. Erlynne in *Fan*, act 3.

Each man sees his own sin in Dorian Gray. What Dorian Gray's sins are no one knows. He who finds them has brought them.

> *Letters*, 266.
> Written to the Editor, *Scots Observer*, on July 9, 1890 in defense of *Dorian Gray*.

Sins of the flesh are nothing. They are maladies for physicians to cure, if they should be cured. Sins of the soul alone are shameful.

> *Letters*, 452.
> Written to Alfred Douglas in early 1897 from Reading Prison, partly pub. as *De Profundis* (1905).

SINCERITY

A little sincerity is a dangerous thing, and a great deal of it is absolutely fatal. The true critic will, indeed, always be sincere in his devotion to the principle of beauty, but he will seek for beauty in every age and in each school, and will never suffer himself to be limited to any settled custom of thought, or stereotyped mode of looking at things.

Gilbert in "The Critic as Artist," pt. 2, in *Intentions* (1891), repr. in Ellmann, 393.

The first sentence borrows Alexander Pope's line in *An Essay on Criticism* (1711): "A little learning is a dangerous thing."

Now, the value of an idea has nothing whatsoever to do with the sincerity of the man who expresses it. Indeed, the probabilities are that the more insincere the man is, the more purely intellectual will the idea be, as in that case it will not coloured by either his wants, his desires, or his prejudices.

Lord Henry in *Dorian Gray*, ch. 1.

SKEPTICISM

Scepticism is the beginning of Faith.

Lord Henry in *Dorian Gray*, ch. 17.

SLAVERY

JIM VANE: He wants to enslave you.
SIBYL VANE: I shudder at the thought of being free.

Dorian Gray, ch. 5.

Brother and sister discuss Dorian.

SOCIALISM

It will, of course, be said that such a scheme [(anarchistic socialism)] as is set forth here is quite unpractical, and goes against human nature. This is perfectly true. It is unpractical, and it goes against human nature. This is why it is worth carrying out, and that is why one proposes it.

"The Soul of Man," repr. in Ellmann, 284.

The chief advantage that would result from the establishment of Socialism is, undoubtedly, the fact that Socialism would relieve us from that sordid necessity of living for others which, in the present condition of things, presses so hardly upon almost everybody.

"The Soul of Man," repr. in Ellmann, 255.

I think I am rather more than a Socialist. I am something of an Anarchist, I believe; but, of course, the dynamite policy is very absurd indeed.

Quoted in: Percival Almy's "New Views of Mr. Oscar Wilde," *Theatre* (March 1894), repr. in Mikhail 1:232.

SOCIETY

Society often forgives the criminal; it never forgives the dreamer. The beautiful sterile emotions that art excites in us, are hateful in its eyes, and so completely are people dominated by the tyranny of this dreadful social ideal that they are always coming shamelessly up to one at Private Views and other places that are open to the general public, and saying in a loud stentorian voice, "What are you doing?" whereas "What are you thinking?" is the only question any single civilized being should ever be allowed to whisper to another.

Gilbert in "The Critic as Artist," pt. 2, in *Intentions* (1891), repr. in Ellmann, 380-81.

While, in the opinion of society, Contemplation is the gravest sin of which any citizen can be guilty, in the opinion of the highest culture it is the proper occupation of man.

Gilbert in "The Critic as Artist," pt. 2, in *Intentions* (1891), repr. in Ellmann, 381.

Never speak disrespectfully of Society, Algernon. Only people who can't get into it do that.

Lady Bracknell in *Earnest*, act 3.

We must first note that the primary cause of the decay of the ideal state is the general principle, common to the vegetable and animal worlds as well as to the world of history, that all created things are fated to decay. . . .

"Historical Criticism," pt. 4.

LORD CAVERSHAM: Can't make out how you stand London Society. The thing has gone to the dogs, a lot of damned nobodies talking about nothing.

LORD GORING: I love talking about nothing, father. It is the only thing I know anything about.

Husband, act 1.

Oh, I love London Society! I think it has immensely improved. It is entirely composed now of beautiful idiots and brilliant lunatics. Just what Society should be.

Mabel Chiltern in *Husband*, act 1.

GERALD: I suppose society is wonderfully delightful!

LORD ILLINGWORTH: To be in it is merely a bore. But to be out of it simply a tragedy. Society is a necessary thing. No man has any real success in this world unless he has got women to back him, and women rule society.

A Woman, act 3.

One's regret is that society should be constructed on such a basis that man has been forced into a groove in which he cannot freely develop what is wonderful, and fascinating, and delightful in him—in which, in fact, he misses the true pleasure and joy of living.

"The Soul of Man," repr. in Ellmann, 261.

The proper aim is to try and reconstruct society on such a basis that poverty will be impossible.

"The Soul of Man," repr. in Ellmann, 256.

To get into the best society, nowadays, one has either to feed people, amuse people, or shock people—that is all.

Lord Illingworth in *A Woman*, act 3.

SORROW

And feeling, with the artistic nature of one to whom Sorrow and Suffering were modes through which he could realise his conception of the Beautiful, that an idea is of no value till it becomes incarnate and is made an image, [Christ] makes of himself the image of the Man of Sorrows, and as such has fascinated and dominated Art as no Greek god ever succeeded in doing.

> *Letters*, 481.
>
> Written to Alfred Douglas in early 1897 from Reading Prison, partly pub. as *De Profundis* (1905).

I now see that sorrow, being the supreme emotion of which man is capable, is at once the type and test of all great Art. What the artist is always looking for is that mode of existence in which soul and body are one and indivisible: in which the outward is expressive of the inward: in which Form reveals.

> *Letters*, 473.
>
> Written to Alfred Douglas in early 1897 from Reading Prison, partly pub. as *De Profundis* (1905).

SOUL, THE

To spiritualize one's age—that is something worth doing. If this girl can give a soul to those who have lived without one, if she can create the sense of beauty in people whose lives have been sordid and ugly, if she can strip them of their selfishness and lend them tears for sorrows that are not their own, she is worthy of all your adoration, worthy of the adoration of the world.

> Lord Henry to Dorian in *Dorian Gray*, ch. 7.
>
> Commenting on the potential effects of Sibyl Vane's acting.

Soul and body, body and soul—how mysterious they were! There was animalism in the soul, and the body had its moments of spirituality. The senses could refine, and the intellect could degrade. Who could say where the fleshly impulse ceased, or the psychical impulse began? How shallow were the arbitrary definitions of ordinary psychologists!

> *Dorian Gray*, ch. 4.
>
> Lord Henry on ultimate mysteries.

Your slim gilt soul walks between passion and poetry.

Letters, 326.

Written to the poet Alfred Douglas in January 1893, a letter introduced into Wilde's trials in 1895.

Those who see any difference between soul and body have neither.

"Phrases and Philosophies," repr. in Ellmann, 433.

*S*PECTATOR

It is the spectator, and not life, that art really mirrors.

Dorian Gray, Preface.

*S*PECULATION

[Dorian] felt keenly conscious of how barren all intellectual speculation is when separated from action and experiment. He knew that the senses, no less than the soul, have their spiritual mysteries to reveal.

Dorian Gray, ch. 11.

*S*PIRITUALITY

We might make ourselves spiritual by detaching ourselves from action, and become perfect by the rejection of energy. It has often seemed to me that Browning felt something of this. Shakespeare hurls Hamlet into active life, and makes him realize his mission by effort. Browning might have given us a Hamlet who would have realized his mission by thought. Incident and event were to him unreal or unmeaning. He made the soul the protagonist of life's tragedy, and looked on action as the one undramatic element of a play.

Gilbert in "The Critic as Artist," pt. 2, in *Intentions* (1891), repr. in Ellmann, 384-85.

Wilde alludes to Browning's play *A Soul's Tragedy* (1846).

*S*T. FRANCIS OF ASSISI

Like dear St. Francis of Assisi I am wedded to Poverty: but in my case the marriage is not a success; I hate the bride that has been given to me. I see no beauty in her hunger and her rags: I have not the soul of St. Francis: my thirst is for the beauty of life: my desire for the joy.

Letters, 803.
Written to the novelist Frances Forbes-Robertson in June 1899.

*S*TARING

He had that dislike of being stared at which comes on geniuses late in life, and never leaves the commonplace.

Dorian Gray, ch. 5.
Jim Vane, Sibyl's brother, here described.

*S*TATE, THE

The State is to be a voluntary association that will organize labour, and be the manufacturer and distributor of necessary commodities. *The State is to make what is useful. The individual is to make what is beautiful.*

"The Soul of Man," repr. in Ellmann, 268.
Wilde's conception of anarchistic Socialism.

*S*TEVENSON, ROBERT LOUIS

Even Mr. Robert Louis Stevenson, that delightful master of delicate and fanciful prose, is tainted with this modern vice [of worshipping facts]. . . . There is such a thing as robbing a story of its reality by trying to make it too true, and *The Black Arrow* is so inartistic as not to contain a single anachronism to boast of, while the transformation of Dr. Jekyll reads dangerously like an experiment out of the *Lancet*.

Vivian in "The Decay of Lying," in *Intentions* (1891), repr. in Ellmann, 295.
The *Lancet* is the British medical journal.

STUPIDITY

Our splendid physique as a people is entirely due to our national stupidity.
I only hope we shall be able to keep this great historic bulwark of our
happiness for many years to come; but I am afraid that we are beginning to
be over-educated; at least everybody who is incapable of learning has taken
to teaching. . . .

Vivian in "The Decay of Lying," in *Intentions* (1891), repr. in Ellmann, 291.

Whenever a man does a thoroughly stupid thing, it is always from the
noblest motives.

Lord Henry in *Dorian Gray*, ch. 6.

STYLE

It is style that makes us believe in a thing—nothing but style. Most of our
modern portrait painters are doomed to absolute oblivion. They never
paint what they see. They paint what the public sees, and the public never
sees anything.

Vivian in "The Decay of Lying," in *Intentions* (1891), repr. in Ellmann, 316.

The new age is the age of style. The same spirit of exclusive attention to
form which made Euripides often, like Swinburne, prefer music to
meaning and melody to morality, which gave to the later Greek statues that
refined effeminacy, that overstrained gracefulness of attitude, was felt in
the sphere of history.

"Historical Criticism," pt. 4.

SUCCESS

Look at the successful men in any of the learned professions. How perfectly
hideous they are! Except, of course, in the Church. But then in the Church
they don't think. A bishop keeps on saying at the age of eighty what he was
told to say when he was a boy of eighteen, and as a natural consequence he
always looks absolutely delightful.

Lord Henry in *Dorian Gray*, ch. 1.

On the effect of intellect on one's appearance.

Suffering

Suffering—curious as it may sound to you—is the means by which we exist, because it is the only means by which we become conscious of existing. . . .

Letters, 435.

Written to Alfred Douglas in early 1897 from Reading Prison, partly pub. as *De Profundis* (1905).

And all the woe that moved him so
That he gave that bitter cry,
And the wild regrets, and the bloody sweats,
None knew so well as I:
For he who lives more lives than one
More deaths than one must die.

Reading Gaol, lines 391-96, repr. in *Poems* (1997).

Following the allusion to the trooper's execution, Wilde's pun on his own name and the lines following imply autobiographical significance.

Suicide

In the present case, what is it that has really happened? Some one has killed herself for love of you. I wish that I had ever had such an experience. It would have made me in love with love for the rest of my life.

Lord Henry to Dorian in *Dorian Gray*, ch. 8.

On Sibyl Vane's suicide.

Sunset

Yesterday evening Mrs. Arundel insisted on my going to the window, and looking at the glorious sky, as she called it. Of course I had to look at it. . . . And what was it? It was simply a very second-rate Turner, a Turner of a bad period, with all the painter's worst faults exaggerated and overemphasized.

Vivian in "The Decay of Lying," in *Intentions* (1891), repr. in Ellmann, 313.

Mrs. Arundel is undoubtedly Wilde's little joke: the Earl of Arundel was a noted 17th-century art collector, and the Arundel Society, founded by John Ruskin, a supporter of Turner, reproduced the works of famous artists.

SUPERFICIALITY

It is the only the superficial qualities that last. Man's deeper nature is soon found out.

"Phrases and Philosophies," repr. in Ellmann, 434.

SUPERSTITION

I love superstitions. They are the colour element of thought and imagination. They are the opponents of common sense. Common sense is the enemy of romance.

Letters, 349.
Written to the actor William H. Blanch in January 1894.

SURPRISE

I am always astonishing myself. It is the only thing that makes life worth living.

Lord Illingworth in *A Woman*, act 3.

SURVIVAL

One can survive everything nowadays, except death, and live down anything except a good reputation.

Lord Illingworth in *A Woman*, act 1.

SUSPENSE

This suspense is terrible. I hope it will last.

Gwendolen in *Earnest*, act 3.
Upstairs, Jack Worthing is noisily searching for the handbag.

SWINBURNE, ALGERNON CHARLES

[Swinburne] has always been a great poet. But he has his limitations, the chief of which is, curiously enough, the entire lack of any sense of limit. His song is nearly always too loud for his subject. His magnificent rhetoric, nowhere more magnificent than in the volume that now lies before us, conceals rather than reveals. It has been said of him, and with truth, that he is a master of language, but with still greater truth it may be said that Language is his master. . . . Mere sound often becomes his lord. He is so eloquent that whatever he touches becomes unreal.

"Mr. Swinburne's Last Volume," in *PMG* (June 27, 1889), repr. in Ellmann, 146.

A review of *Poems and Ballads,* Third Series.

SWITZERLAND

I don't like Switzerland: it has produced nothing but theologians and waiters.

Letters, 787.

Written to Louis Wilkinson, a Radley student, in March 1899 from Switzerland.

SYMPATHY

I can sympathize with everything, except suffering. I cannot sympathize with that. It is too ugly, too horrible, too distressing. There is something terribly morbid in the modern sympathy with pain. One should sympathize with the colour, the beauty, the joy of life. The less said about life's sores the better.

Lord Henry in *Dorian Gray,* ch. 3; in *A Woman,* act 1, Lord Illingworth has a briefer version of the passage, and in *Earnest,* act 1, Lady Bracknell echoes Lord Henry's.

I am quite content with philosophic contemplation. But, as the nineteenth century has gone bankrupt through an over-expenditure of sympathy, I would suggest that we should appeal to Science to put us straight.

Lord Henry in *Dorian Gray,* ch. 3.

LORD CAVERSHAM: Oh, damn sympathy. There is a great deal too much of that sort of thing going on nowadays.
LORD GORING: I quite agree with you, father. If there was less sympathy in the world there would be less trouble in the world.
LORD CAVERSHAM: That is a paradox, sir. I hate paradoxes.
LORD GORING: So do I, father. Everybody one meets is a paradox nowadays. It is a great bore. It makes society so obvious.

Husband, act 3.

There is not a single colour hidden away in the chalice of a flower, or the curve of a shell, to which, by some subtle sympathy with the very soul of things, my nature does not answer. . . . I am conscious now that behind all this Beauty, satisfying though it be, there is some Spirit hidden of which the painted forms and shapes are but modes of manifestation, and it is with this Spirit that I desire to become in harmony.

Letters, 509.
Written to Alfred Douglas in early 1897 from Reading Prison, partly pub. as De Profundis (1905).

One should sympathize with the entirety of life, not with life's sores and maladies merely, but with life's joy and beauty and energy and health and freedom. The wider sympathy is, of course, the more difficult. It requires more unselfishness. Anybody can sympathize with the sufferings of a friend, but it requires a very fine nature—it requires, in fact, the nature of a true Individualist—to sympathize with a friend's success.

"The Soul of Man," repr. in Ellmann, 286.

TALKING

Don't talk about horrid subjects. If one doesn't talk about a thing, it has never happened. It is simply expression, as Harry says, that gives reality to things.

Dorian to Basil Hallward in Dorian Gray, ch. 9.

Talking to him was like playing upon an exquisite violin. He answered to every touch and thrill of the bow. . . .

Dorian Gray, ch. 3.
Lord Henry musing on Dorian's responsiveness.

Wonderful woman, Lady Markby, isn't she? Talks more and says less than anybody I ever met. She is made to be a public speaker. Much more so than her husband, though he is a typical Englishman, always dull and usually violent.

Mrs. Cheveley in *Husband*, act 2.

*T*EMPERAMENT

There are certain temperaments that marriage makes more complex. They retain their egotism, and add to it many other egos. They are forced to have more than one life. They become more highly organized, and to be highly organized is, I should fancy, the object of man's existence.

Lord Henry in *Dorian Gray*, ch. 6.

*T*EMPTATION

Every impulse that we strive to strangle broods in the mind and poisons us. The body sins once, and has done with its sin, for action is a mode of purification. . . . The only way to rid of temptation is to yield to it. Resist it, and your soul grows sick with longing for the things it has forbidden to itself. . . .

Lord Henry in *Dorian Gray*, ch. 2, the passage echoed in Lord Darlington's line in *Fan*, act 1: "I can resist everything except temptation."

The capacity of finding temptations is the test of the culture of one's nature. The capacity of yielding to temptations is the test of the strength of one's character.

Quoted in: Small, 142.

There are terrible temptations that it requires strength, strength and courage, to yield to. To stake all one's life on a single moment, to risk everything on one throw, whether the stake be power or pleasure, I care not—there is no weakness in that. There is a horrible, a terrible courage.

Sir Robert Chiltern in *Husband*, act 2.

*T*ERROR

I turned half-way round, and saw Dorian Gray for the first time. When our eyes met, I felt that I was growing pale. A curious sensation of terror came over me. I knew that I had come face to face with some one whose mere personality was so fascinating that, if I allowed it to do so, it would absorb my whole nature, my whole soul, my very art itself.

> Basil Hallward in *Dorian Gray*, ch. 1.

*T*ERRY, *ELLEN*

Methinks I'd rather see thee play
That serpent of old Nile, whose witchery
Made Emperors drunken,—come, great Egypt, shake
Our stage with all thy mimic pageants! Nay,
I am grown sick of unreal passions, make
The world thine Actium, me thine Antony!

> "Camma," in *Poems* (1881), repr. in *Poems* (1997).
>
> This poem was written for Ellen Terry, who performed the role of Camma, a priestess of the virgin goddess of the hunt, Artemis, in Tennyson's *The Cup* (1881); the "serpent of old Nile" is Shakespeare's Cleopatra in *Antony and Cleopatra*, act 1, sc. 5; in the fifth line above, Wilde modifies a line from Tennyson's poem "The Lady of Shalott": "I am half sick of shadows," which Wilde also borrows for *Dorian Gray*, ch. 7, when Sibyl Vane says: "I have grown sick of shadows."

*T*HEATER

The stage is not merely the meeting place of all the arts, but is also the return of art to life.

> "The Truth of Masks," in *Intentions* (1891), repr. in Ellmann, 417.

*T*HEORIES

DORIAN: Oh, your theories about life, your theories about love, your theories about pleasure. . . .

LORD HENRY: Pleasure is the only thing worth having a theory about.

> *Dorian Gray*, ch. 6.

TOWN

When one is in town one amuses oneself. When one is in the country one amuses other people. It is excessively boring.

Jack Worthing in *Earnest*, act 1.

The first indication in the play of Jack's double life.

TRAGEDIES

The mimic spectacle of life that Tragedy affords cleanses the bosom of much "perilous stuff," and by presenting high and worthy objects for the exercise of the emotions purifies and spiritualizes the man; nay, not merely does it spiritualize him, but it initiates him also into noble feeling of which he might else have known nothing. . . .

Gilbert in "The Critic as Artist," pt. 1, in *Intentions* (1891), repr. in Ellmann, 353.

Aristotle's concept of catharsis, interpreted here, is associated by Wilde with cleansing the "stuff'd bosom of that perilous stuff" in Lady Macbeth (*Macbeth*, act 5, sc. 3).

One of the greatest tragedies of my life is the death of Lucien de Rubempré. It is a grief from which I have never been able to completely rid myself. It haunts me in my moments of pleasure. I remember it when I laugh.

Vivian in "The Decay of Lying," in *Intentions* (1891), repr. in Ellmann, 299.

Lucien de Rubempré, the impoverished young poet who kills himself, appears in Balzac's *Les Illusions perdues* (1837-43) and in *Splendeurs et misères des courtisanes* (1845).

It often happens that the real tragedies of life occur in such an inartistic manner that they hurt us by their crude violence, their absolute incoherence, their absurd want of meaning, their entire lack of style. . . . They give us an impression of sheer brute force, and we revolt against that.

Lord Henry in *Dorian Gray*, ch. 8.

Remarks prompted by the suicide of Sibyl Vane.

I should fancy that the real tragedy of the poor is that they can afford nothing but self-denial. Beautiful sins, like beautiful things, are the privilege of the rich.

Lord Henry in *Dorian Gray*, ch. 6.

In this world there are only two tragedies. One is not getting what one wants, and the other is getting it. The last is much the worst, the last is a real tragedy!

Dumby in *Fan*, act 3.

There is only one real tragedy in a woman's life. The fact that her past is always her lover, and her future invariably her husband.

Mrs. Cheveley in *Husband*, act 3.

Everything about my tragedy has been hideous, mean, repellent, lacking in style.

Letters, 490.
Written to Alfred Douglas in May 1897 from Reading Prison, partly pub. as *De Profundis* (1905).

I used to say that I thought I could bear a real tragedy if it came to me with purple pall and a mask of noble sorrow, but that the dreadful thing about modernity was that it put Tragedy into the raiment of Comedy, so that the great realities seemed commonplace or grotesque or lacking in style.

Letters, 490.
Written to Alfred Douglas in early 1897 from Reading Prison, partly pub. as *De Profundis* (1905).

No man of my position can fall into the mire of life without getting a great deal of pity from his inferiors; and I know that when plays last too long, spectators tire. *My* tragedy has lasted far too long: its climax is over: its end is mean; and I am quite conscious of the fact that when the end *does* come I shall return an unwelcome visitant to a world that does not want me. . . .

Letters, 413.
Written to Robert Ross in November 1896 from Reading Prison.

*T*RANSCENDENTALISM

This spirit of transcendentalism [is] alien to the spirit of art. For the artist can accept no sphere of life in exchange for life itself. For him there is no escape from the bondage of the earth: there is not even the desire of escape.

"English Renaissance," pub. in *Miscellanies*, 248.

TRAVEL

From Salt Lake City one travels over the great plains of Colorado and up the Rocky Mountains, on the top of which is Leadville, the richest city in the world. It has also got the reputation of being the roughest, and every man carries a revolver. I was told that if I went there they would be sure to shoot me or my travelling manager. I wrote and told them that nothing that they could do to my travelling manager would intimidate me.

Impressions of America, ed. Stuart Mason (Sunderland, 1906), repr. in Ellmann, 9.

TRIALS

All trials are trials for one's life, just as all sentences are sentences of death, and three times have I been tried.

Letters, 509-10.

Written to Alfred Douglas in early 1897 from Reading Prison, partly pub. as De Profundis (1905).

TRIVIALITY

The trivial in thought and action is charming. I had made it the keystone of a very brilliant philosophy expressed in plays and paradoxes.

Letters, 432.

Written to Alfred Douglas in early 1897 from Reading Prison, partly pub. as De Profundis (1905).

TRUTH

Gwendolen, it is a terrible thing for a man to find out suddenly that all his life he has been speaking nothing but the truth.

Jack Worthing in Earnest, act 3.

Jack has discovered that his name is really Ernest.

Gwendolen—Cecily—it is very painful for me to be forced to speak the truth. It is the first time in my life that I have ever been reduced to such a painful position, and I am really quite inexperienced in doing anything of the kind. . . . I have no brother at all. I never had a brother in my life, and I certainly have not the smallest intention of ever having one in the future.

Jack Worthing in *Earnest*, act 2.
Jack's confession when confronted by the two women engaged to "Ernest."

JACK: That, my dear Algy, is the whole truth pure and simple.
ALGERNON: The truth is rarely pure and never simple. Modern life would be very tedious if it were either, and modern literature a complete impossibility!

Earnest, act 1.

Truth in Art is the unity of a thing with itself: the outward rendered expressive of the inward: the soul made incarnate: the body instinct with spirit. For this reason there is no truth comparable to Sorrow.

Letters, 473.
Written to Alfred Douglas in early 1897 from Reading Prison, partly pub. as *De Profundis* (1905).

A truth ceases to be true when more than one person believes in it.

"Phrases and Philosophies," repr. in Ellmann, 434.

If one tells the truth, one is sure, sooner or later, to be found out.

"Phrases and Philosophies," repr. in Ellmann, 433.

The essay simply represents an artistic standpoint, and in aesthetic criticism attitude is everything. For in art there is no such thing as a universal truth. A Truth in art is that whose contradictory is also true.

"The Truth of Masks," in *Intentions* (1891), repr. in Ellmann, 432.

The things about which one feels absolutely certain are never true. That is the fatality of Faith, and the lesson of Romance.

Quoted in: Small, 131.

TURGENEV, IVAN

Of the three great Russian novelists of our time Tourgenieff is by far the finest artist. He has that spirit of exquisite selection, that delicate choice of detail, which is the essence of style; his work is entirely free from any personal intention; and by taking existence at its most fiery-coloured moments he can distil into a few pages of perfect prose the moods and passions of many lives.

"A Batch of Novels," in *PMG* (May 2, 1887), repr. in *Reviews*, 157.

The other two Russian novelists alluded to are Tolstoy and Dostoevsky.

UGLINESS

The ugly and the stupid have the best of it in this world. They can sit at their ease and gape at the play. If they know nothing of victory, they are at least spared the knowledge of defeat. They live as we all should live, undisturbed, indifferent, and without disquiet. They neither bring ruin upon others, nor ever receive it from alien hands.

Basil Hallward in *Dorian Gray*, ch. 1.

DUCHESS OF MONMOUTH: Ugliness is one of the seven deadly sins, then?
LORD HENRY: Ugliness is one of the seven deadly virtues, Gladys. You, as a
   good Tory, must not underrate them. Beer, the Bible, and the seven
   deadly virtues have made our England what she is.

Dorian Gray, ch. 17.

Hesketh Pearson quotes Sydney Smith (1771-1845) in *The Smith of Smiths* (1934), ch. 13: "What two ideas are more inseparable than Beer and Britannia?"

No object is so ugly that, under certain conditions of light and shade, or proximity to other things, it will not look beautiful; no object is so beautiful that, under certain conditions, it will not look ugly. I believe that in every twenty-four hours what is beautiful looks ugly, and what is ugly looks beautiful, once.

"Lecture to Art Students," of the Royal Academy (June 30, 1883), pub. in *Miscellanies*, 318-19; the passage echoed in "The Relation of Dress to Art: A Note in Black and White on Mr. Whistler's Lecture," *PMG*

(February 28, 1885), repr. in Ellmann, 17-18: . . . "under certain conditions of light and shade, what is ugly in fact may in its effect become beautiful, is true; and this, indeed, is the real *modernité* of art. . . ."

An ugly thing is merely a thing that is badly made, or a thing that does not serve its purpose; that ugliness is want of fitness; that ugliness is failure; that ugliness is uselessness, such as ornament in the wrong place, while beauty . . . is the purgation of superfluities.

"More Radical Ideas upon Dress Reform," in *PMG* (November 11, 1884), repr. in *Miscellanies*, 59.

A FRENCH WOMAN WRITER: Is it not true, Mr. Wilde, that I am the ugliest woman in France?
WILDE: In the world, madame, in the world.

Quoted in: Harris, ch. 20.

Decidedly one of us will have to go.

Quoted in: H. Montgomery Hyde, *Oscar Wilde* (New York, 1975), 226.

Allegedly said by Wilde on his death bed concerning the magenta-flowered wallpaper in his Parisian hotel room.

U*NDERCLASS, THE*

My lords, this age is so familiar grown,
That the low peasant hardly doffs his hat,
Unless you beat him; and the raw mechanic
Elbows the noble in the public streets,
As for this rabble here, I am their scourge,
And sent by God to lash them for their sins.

Duke of Padua in *Duchess*, act 2.

If the lower orders don't set us a good example, what on earth is the use of them? They seem, as a class, to have absolutely no sense of moral responsibility.

Algernon Moncrieff in *Earnest*, act 1.

LORD GORING: Extraordinary thing about the lower classes in England—they are always losing their relations.
PHIPPS: Yes, my lord! They are extremely fortunate in that respect.

Husband, act 3.

There is only one class in the community that thinks more about money than the rich, and that is the poor. The poor can think of nothing else. That is the misery of being poor.

"The Soul of Man," repr. in Ellmann, 264.

We are often told that the poor are grateful for charity. Some of them are, no doubt, *but the best amongst the poor are never grateful.* They are ungrateful, discontented, disobedient, and rebellious. They are quite right to be so. Charity they feel to be a ridiculously inadequate mode of partial restitution, or a sentimental dole, usually accompanied by some impertinent attempt on the part of the sentimentalist to tyrannize over their private lives.

"The Soul of Man," repr. in Ellmann, 258.

UTILITARIANISM

We call ourselves a utilitarian age, and we do not know the uses of any single thing.

Letters, 509.

Written to Alfred Douglas in early 1897 from Reading Prison, partly pub. as *De Profundis* (1905).

UTOPIA

A map of the world that does not include Utopia is not worth even glancing at, for it leaves out the one country at which Humanity is always landing. And when Humanity lands there, it looks out, and, seeing a better country, sets sail. Progress is the realisation of Utopias.

"The Soul of Man," repr. in Ellmann, 270-71.

The term *utopia* (Greek: "nowhere") first appeared in Sir Thomas More's *Utopia* (1516) as a designation of an ideal state.

$\mathcal{V}$ANITY

Nothing makes one so vain as being told that one is a sinner. Conscience makes egotists of us all.

Lord Henry in *Dorian Gray*, ch. 8.

An echo of Hamlet's "conscience does make cowards of us all," act 3, sc. 1.

$\mathcal{V}$ENUS DE MILO

So infinitesimal did I find the knowledge of Art, west of the Rocky Mountains, than an art patron—one who in his day had been a miner—actually sued the railroad company for damages because the plaster cast of Venus of Milo, which he had imported from Paris, had been delivered minus the arms. And, what is more surprising still, he gained his case and the damages.

Impressions of America, ed. Stuart Mason (Sunderland, 1906), repr. in Ellmann, 10.

$\mathcal{V}$ISION

One does not see anything until one sees its beauty. Then, and then only, does it come into existence.

Vivian in "The Decay of Lying," in *Intentions* (1891), repr. in Ellmann, 312.

$\mathcal{W}$AGNER, RICHARD

[Dorian] would sit in his box at the opera, either alone or with Lord Henry, listening in rapt pleasure to "Tannhäuser" and seeing in the prelude to that great work of art a presentation of the tragedy of his own soul.

Dorian Gray, ch. 11.

I like Wagner's music better than anybody's. It is so loud that one can talk the whole time without other people hearing what one says.

Lady Henry in *Dorian Gray*, ch. 4.

$\mathcal{W}$AINEWRIGHT, THOMAS GRIFFITHS

It is only the Philistine who seeks to estimate a personality by the vulgar test of production. This young dandy [Wainewright] sought to be somebody, rather than to do something. He recognized that Life itself is an art, and has its modes of style no less than the arts that seek to express it.

"Pen, Pencil, and Poison," in *Intentions* (1891), repr. in Ellmann, 324.

[Wainewright] had that curious love of green, which in individuals is always the sign of a subtle artistic temperament, and in nations is said to denote a laxity, if not a decadence of morals.

"Pen, Pencil, and Poison," in *Intentions* (1891), repr. in Ellmann, 324.

In the late 19th century, green was associated with Decadence; on occasion, Wilde wore a carnation dyed green, at once natural and artificial.

$\mathcal{W}$AITING

JACK: I must retire to my room for a moment. Gwendolen, wait here for me.
GWENDOLEN: If you are not too long, I will wait here for you all my life.

Earnest, act 3.

$\mathcal{W}$AR

Here have our wild war-eagles flown,
And flapped wide wings in fiery fight;
But the sad dove, that sits alone
In England—she hath no delight.

"Ave Imperatrix," lines 57-60, in *The World* (August 25, 1880), repr. in *Poems* (1997).

At this time, Britain was at war with Afghanistan;, the "sad dove," presumably Queen Victoria, was opposed to the "war-eagles."

As long as war is regarded as wicked, it will have its fascination. When it is looked upon as vulgar, it will cease to be popular.

> Gilbert in "The Critic as Artist," pt. 2, in *Intentions* (1891), repr. in Ellmann, 405.

WATSON, WILLIAM

There is not enough fire in William Watson's poetry to boil a tea-kettle.

> Quoted in: Percival Almay's "New Views of Mr. Oscar Wilde," *Theatre* (March 1894), repr. in Mikhail 1:230.
>
> Watson had written satirical verse after Wilde threatened to become a French citizen because his *Salomé* had been refused a license for the stage.

WEAK, THE

Only the weak resist temptation.

> Quoted in: Small, 142.

WEALTH

I do not approve of mercenary marriages. When I married Lord Bracknell I had no fortune of any kind. But I never dreamed for a moment of allowing that to stand in my way.

> Lady Bracknell in *Earnest*, act 3.

WEARINESS

O we are wearied of this sense of guilt,
Wearied of pleasure's paramour despair,
Wearied of every temple we have built,
Wearied of every right, unanswered, prayer,
For man is weak; God sleeps: and heaven is high:
One fiery-coloured moment: one great love; and lo! we die.

> "Panthea," lines 79-84, in *Poems* (1881), repr. in *Poems* (1997).

*W*EATHER, *THE*

GWENDOLEN: Pray don't talk to me about the weather, Mr. Worthing. Whenever people talk to me about the weather, I always feel quite certain that they mean something else. And that makes me so nervous.
JACK: I do mean something else.
GWENDOLEN: I thought so. In fact, I am never wrong.

> *Earnest*, act 1.

*W*ESTERN *WORLD*

While the Western world has been laying on art the intolerable burden of its own intellectual doubts and the spiritual tragedy of its own sorrows, the East has always kept true to art's primary and pictorial conditions.

> "English Renaissance," pub. in *Miscellanies*, 260-61.
>
> In his lecture, Wilde stresses "the fascination of all Japanese work."

*W*HISTLER, *JAMES MCNEILL*

Indeed, when the true history of Art comes to be written, a task that Mr. Whistler is eminently capable of doing himself, at least in the form of an autobiography, there can be no doubt but that his name will stand high amongst the highest on its record, for he has opened the eyes of the blind, and given great encouragement to the short-sighted.

> "The Butterfly's Boswell," in *CSR*(April 21, 1887), repr. in Ellmann, 67.
>
> Whistler's "Boswell" was Walter Dowdeswell, who had published a biographical article in the *Art Journal* (April 1887).

Mr. Whistler has recently done two rooms in London which are marvels of beauty. One is the famous Peacock Room, which I regard as the finest thing in colour and art decoration that the world has known since Correggio painted that wonderful room in Italy where the little children are dancing on the walls; everything is of the colours in peacock's feathers, and each part so coloured with regard to the whole that the room, when lighted up, seems like a great peacock tail spread out.

> "The House Beautiful," in O'Brien, 169.
>
> The Peacock Room is now in the Freer Art Gallery, Washington, DC.

Mr. Whistler was relentless, and, with charming ease and much grace of manner, explained to the public that the only thing they should cultivate was ugliness, and that on their permanent stupidity rested all the hopes of art in the future.

> "Mr. Whistler's Ten O'Clock," in *PMG* (February 21, 1885), repr. in Ellmann, 14.
> On Whistler's lecture on art.

Mr. Whistler's lecture last night was, like everything that he does, a masterpiece. Not merely for its clever satire and amusing jests will it be remembered, but for the pure and perfect beauty of many of its passages— passages delivered with an earnestness which seemed to amaze those who had looked on Mr. Whistler as a master of persiflage merely. . . .

> "Mr. Whistler's Ten O'Clock," in *PMG* (February 21, 1885), repr. in Ellmann, 15-16.
> On Whistler's lecture on art.

Having thus made a holocaust of humanity, Mr. Whistler turned to Nature, and in a few moments convicted her of the Crystal Palace, Bank holidays, and . . . spoke of the artistic value of dim dawns and dusks, when the mean facts of life are lost in exquisite and evanescent effects, when common things are touched with mystery and transfigured with beauty; when the warehouses become as palaces, and the tall chimneys of the factory seem like campaniles in the silver air.

> "Mr. Whistler's Ten O'Clock," in *PMG* (February 21, 1885), repr. in Ellmann, 14-15.
> Whistler's lecture on art; in "The Decay of Lying," in *Intentions* (1891), Wilde mimics Whistler's view of the transforming imagination: see Ellmann, 312.

The scene was in every way delightful; he stood there, a miniature Mephistopheles, mocking the majority! he was like a brilliant surgeon lecturing to a class composed of subjects destined ultimately for dissection, and solemnly assuring them how valuable to science their maladies were, and how absolutely uninteresting the slightest symptoms of health on their part would be.

> "Mr. Whistler's Ten O'Clock," in *PMG* (February 21, 1885), repr. in Ellmann, 14.
> Whistler's lecture on art.

Mr. Whistler always spelt art, and we believe still spells it, with a capital "I." However, he was never dull. His brilliant wit, his caustic satire, and his amusing epigrams, or perhaps we should say epitaphs on his contemporaries made his views on art as delightful as they were misleading, and as fascinating as they were unsound. Besides, he introduced humour into art criticism, and for this if for no other reason he deserves to be affectionately remembered.

"The New President," *PMG* (January 26, 1889), repr. in Ellmann, 126.

A review of Wyke Bayliss's *The Enchanged Island* (Bayliss, a member of the Royal Society of British Artists, had replaced Whistler as the new president).

Popularity is the only insult that has not yet been offered to Mr. Whistler.

Quoted in: Whistler's *The Gentle Art of Making Enemies* (2nd ed., 1892; repr. New York, 1967), 99.

Whitman, walt

Certainly in Walt Whitman's views there is a largeness of vision, a healthy sanity, and a fine ethical purpose. He is not to be placed with the professional *littérateurs* of his country, Boston novelists, New York poets, and the like. He stands apart, and the chief value of his work is in its prophecy not in its performance. . . . He is the herald to a new era. As a man he is the precursor of a fresh type. . . . He is a factor in the heroic and spiritual evolution of the human being.

"The Gospel According to Walt Whitman," *PMG* (January 25, 1889), repr. in Ellmann, 125.

Wickedness

LADY NARBOROUGH: Everybody I know says you are very wicked. . . .

LORD HENRY: It is perfectly monstrous the way people go about nowadays saying things against one behind one's back that are absolutely and entirely true.

Dorian Gray, ch. 15; Lord Henry's response is echoed by Lord Illingworth in *A Woman*, act 1.

LADY NARBOROUGH: Lord Henry, I am not at all surprised that the world says that you are extremely wicked.

LORD HENRY: But what world says that? It can only be the next world. This world and I are on excellent terms.

Dorian Gray, ch. 15; Lord Henry's response is later used by Lord Illingworth in *A Woman*, act 1.

ALGERNON: Oh! I am not really wicked at all, Cousin Cecily. You musn't think that I am wicked.

CECILY: If you are not, then you have certainly been deceiving us all in a very inexcusable manner. I hope you have not been leading a double life, pretending to be wicked and being really good all the time. That would be hypocrisy.

    Earnest, act 2.

As a wicked man I am a complete failure. Why, there are lots of people who say I have never really done anything wrong in the whole course of my life. Of course they only say it behind my back.

    Lord Darlington in *Fan*, act 1.

I have never met any really wicked person. I feel rather frightened. I am so afraid he will look just like everyone else. *Enter ALGERNON, very gay and debonnair*. He does!

    Cecily Cardew in *Earnest*, act 2.

    Algernon here pretends to be Jack's wicked brother, Ernest.

Wickedness is a myth invented by good people to account for the curious attractiveness of others.

    "Phrases and Philosophies," repr. in Ellmann, 433.

*W*ILD *OATS*

I have never sowed wild oats: I have planted a few orchids.

    Quoted in: Small, 144.

    Apparently written for use in a play.

*W*INTER, *JOHN STRANGE*

We would earnestly beg "Mr. Winter" not to write foolish prefaces about unappreciative critics; for it is only mediocrities and old maids who consider it a grievance to be misunderstood.

    "Some Novels," *Saturday Review* (May 7, 1887), repr. in *Reviews*, 167.

    A review of *That Imp* by "John Strange Winter," the pseudonym of Mrs. Arthur Stannard.

Women

DUCHESS OF MONMOUTH: Describe us as a sex.
LORD HENRY: Sphinxes without secrets.

> *Dorian Gray*, ch. 17.
>
> Wilde's story "Lady Alroy," in *The World* (May 25, 1887), was reprinted as "The Sphinx without a Secret" in *Lord Arthur*; Lord Henry's remark reappears as Lord Illingworth's in *A Woman*, act 1.

I am afraid that women appreciate cruelty, downright cruelty, more than anything else. They have wonderfully primitive instincts. We have emancipated them, but they remain slaves looking for their masters, all the same. They love being dominated.

> Lord Henry in *Dorian Gray*, ch. 8.

Women are wonderfully practical, much more practical than we are. In situations of that kind we often forget to say anything about marriage, and they always remind us.

> Lord Henry in *Dorian Gray*, ch. 6.

Do you remember saying that women's love
Turns men to angels? well, the love of man
Turns women into martyrs; for its sake
We do or suffer anything.

> Duchess in *Duchess*, act 3.
>
> For the love of Guido Ferrante, the Duchess has just killed her husband.

JACK: Cecily and Gwendolen are perfectly certain to be extremely great friends. I'll bet you anything you like that half an hour after they have met, they will be calling each other sister.
ALGERNON: Women only do that when they have called each other a lot of other things first.

> *Earnest*, act 1.

The amount of women in London who flirt with their own husbands is perfectly scandalous. It looks so bad. It is simply washing one's clean linen in public.

> Algernon Moncrieff in *Earnest*, act 1.

I don't think now that people can be divided into the good and the bad, as though they were two separate races or creations. What are called good women may have terrible things in them, mad moods of recklessness, assertion, jealousy, sin. Bad women, as they are termed, may have in them sorrow, repentance, pity, sacrifice.

Lady Windermere in *Fan*, act 4.

London is full of women who trust their husbands. One can always recognize them. They look so thoroughly unhappy.

Lady Windermere in *Fan*, act 2.

[Mrs. Cheveley] wore far too much rouge last night, and not quite enough clothes. That is always a sign of despair in a woman.

Lord Goring in *Husband*, act 2.

The history of women is the history of the worst form of tyranny the world has ever known. The tyranny of the weak over the strong. It is the only tyranny that lasts.

Lord Illingworth in *A Woman*, act 3.

The three women I have most admired are Queen Victoria, Sarah Bernhardt, and Lily Langtry. I would have married any one of them with pleasure.

Quoted in: Vincent O'Sullivan, *Aspects of Wilde* (New York, 1936), 18.

Women marry in order to find peace, and take lovers in the hopes of having excitement. In both cases they are disappointed.

Quoted in: Small, 130.

*W*OMEN: *AMERICAN*

LORD FERMOR: Why can't these American women stay in their own
    country? They are always telling us that it is the paradise for women.
LORD HENRY: It is. That is the reason why, like Eve, they are so excessively
    anxious to get out of it.

Dorian Gray, ch. 3; the lines reappear in *A Woman*, act 1.

WORK

Work never seems to me a reality, but a way of getting rid of reality.

Letters, 352.
Written to the poet W. E. Henley in February 1894.

Work is the curse of the drinking classes of this country. . . .

Quoted in: Harris, ch. 11.

WORSHIP

From the moment I met you, your personality had the most extraordinary influence over me. I was dominated, soul, brain, and power by you. You became to me the visible incarnation of that unseen ideal whose memory haunts us artists like an exquisite dream. I worshipped you.

Basil Hallward to Dorian in *Dorian Gray*, ch. 9.

In the earlier edition (1890), Hallward says, "It is quite true that I have worshipped you with far more romance of feeling than a man usually gives to a friend. Somehow, I had never loved a woman."

WRITING: RUSSIAN

Russian writers are extraordinary. What makes their books so great is the pity they put into them. You know how fond I used to be of *Madame Bovary*, but Flaubert would not admit pity into his work, and that is why it has a petty and restrained character about it. It is sense of pity by which a work gains in expanse, and by which it opens up a boundless horizon.

Quoted in: Gide, ch. 3.

WRITING

I write because it gives me the greatest possible artistic pleasure to write. If my work pleases the few, I am gratified. If it does not, it causes me no pain. As for the mob, I have no desire to be a popular novelist. It is far too easy.

Letters, 266.
Written to the Editor, *Scots Observer*, on July 9, 1890 in defense of *Dorian Gray*.

YEATS, WILLIAM BUTLER

Books of poetry by young writers are usually promissory notes that are never met. Now and then, however, one comes across a volume that is so far above the average that one can hardly resist the fascinating temptation of recklessly prophesying a fine future for its author. Such a volume Mr. Yeats's "Wanderings of Oisin" certainly is. Here we find nobility of treatment and nobility of subject matter, delicacy of poetic instinct, and richness of imaginative resource.

"Three New Poets: Yeats, Fitz Gerald, Le Gallienne," in *PMG* (July 12, 1889), the Yeats portion repr. in Ellmann, 150 (the entire review repr. in *Reviews*, 523-27).

YOUTH

Ah! realize your youth while you have it. Don't squander the gold of your days, listening to the tedious, trying to improve the hopeless failures, or giving away your life to the ignorant, the common, and the vulgar. These are the sickly aims, the false ideals of our age.

Lord Henry to Dorian in *Dorian Gray*, ch. 2.

To get back one's youth, one has merely to repeat one's follies.

Lord Henry in *Dorian Gray*, ch. 3.

We never get back our youth. The pulse of joy that beats in us at twenty, becomes sluggish. Our limbs fail, our senses rot. We degenerate into hideous puppets, haunted by the memory of the passions of which we were too much afraid, and the exquisite temptations that we had not the courage to yield to. Youth! Youth! There is absolutely nothing in the world but youth!

Lord Henry to Dorian in *Dorian Gray*, ch. 2.

Ah! it was easy when the world was young
To keep one's life free and inviolate,
From our sad lips another song is rung,
By our own hands our heads are desecrate,
Wanderers in drear exile, and dispossessed
Of what should be our own, we can but feed on wild unrest.

"Humanitad," lines 397-402, in *Poems* (1881), repr. in *Poems* (1997).
Wilde's pun on his own name again suggests autobiography.

To get back my youth I would do anything in the world, except take exercise, get up early, or be respectable.

Lord Henry in *Dorian Gray*, ch. 19, the remark echoed by Lord Illingworth in *A Woman*, act 3.

ZOLA, EMILE

[Zola] is not without power. . . . But his work is entirely wrong from beginning to end, and wrong not on the ground of morals, but on the ground of art. From any ethical standpoint it is just what it should be. The author is perfectly truthful, and describes things exactly as they happen. . . .

Vivian in "The Decay of Lying," in *Intentions* (1891), repr. in Ellmann, 296.

M. Zola's characters . . . have their dreary vices, and their drearier virtues. The record of their lives is absolutely without interest. Who cares what happens to them? In literature we require distinction, charm, beauty, and imaginative power. We don't want to be harrowed and disgusted with an account of the doings of the lower orders.

Vivian in "The Decay of Lying," in *Intentions* (1891), repr. in Ellmann, 296.